PRIEST AND PRIESTESS

by

George William Rutler

TRINITY PRESS
708 BETHLEHEM PIKE, AMBLER, PA.

ACKNOWLEDGEMENT:
We express our grateful appreciation to the various authors and publishers for permission to use material for which appropriate credit is given in the appendix.

COVER DESIGN: Carla Coutts

The Virgin and Child is reprinted by permission of The Metropolitan Museum of Art.

PRIEST AND PRIESTESS
© 1973 by
TRINITY PRESS
708 BETHLEHEM PIKE, AMBLER, PA. 19002
All rights reserved.
Library of Congress Catalog Number: 73-75334
ISBN: 0-912046-09-0
Printed in the United States of America

PRIEST AND PRIESTESS

To my parents

"The point is that unless 'equal' means 'interchangeable,' equality makes nothing for the priesthood of women."

C. S. Lewis

TABLE OF CONTENTS

Chapter I	The Sensible Priesthood	3
Chapter II	Neither Male Nor Female	13
Chapter III	Mud and Diamonds	25
Chapter IV	Our Mother Who Art in Heaven	31
Chapter V	Reaching A Decision	39
Chapter VI	Lambeth	45
Chapter VII	The Bible	55
Chapter VIII	Neither Up Nor Down	65
Chapter IX	The Icon of Christ	77

PREFACE

Anglicanism has long made its claim to be truly Catholic and truly Reformed. Its comprehensiveness has meant much wonder as well as much frustration and frequent suffering. Nevertheless Anglicanism has managed to be a home for many parties. On occasion that domestic order has been threatened: we are reminded of the Non-Jurors, of the defections following the Gorham case, and of the Presbyterian merger discussions of the 1940's among others. The ordination of women would be for many the most dramatic statement that Anglican comprehensiveness can no longer weather the hasty temper of the times. The fact that four hundred years have not seen the Elizabethan Compromise wrecked gives some consolation. The fact that so many seem to think the ordination issue is of secondary importance to the life of the Church gives cause for pessimism.

This short study, while not a formal dissertation, is an attempt to uncover some of the hitherto ignored theological implications of altering the male priesthood. I should not expect all or even most men and women who wish to preserve the historic priesthood within Anglicanism share the particular symbolic arguments I have given in its defense. What is important is that we realize what a weighty matter we are approaching. If we are patient and continue the debate in a reasoned way, the ordination controversy will be a guide to a deeper understanding of ecclesiology and sexuality as we approach the twenty-first century.

I wish to express my appreciation for the thoughtful attention given this study by the Association for Creative Theology. I especially want to record my debt to the Reverend Livingston T. Merchant, Jr., Ph.D. who has guided the completion of this study and who has been a brother priest with me at the schools and hospitals and altars of this parish.

George William Rutler

The Rectory
Rosemont, Pennsylvania
December 20, 1972

ACT — The Association for Creative Theology

This book is a monograph sponsored by the Association for Creative Theology. ACT is an organization of communicants of the Episcopal Church which seeks to promote the discussion of problems of a social and theological nature facing the Church today. The Association seeks to open the discussion to proponents of all views, but at the same time it bases its own positions on the Catholic tradition of Anglican theology and contemporary progressive social thought.

Priest and Priestess is the first of a series of papers and monographs planned by ACT. Anyone interested in supporting this work and becoming a subscriber to future publications should write ACT, One East Twenty-Ninth Street, New York, New York, 10016.

Chapter 1

THE SENSIBLE PRIESTHOOD

As the Armada pointed at England, Elizabeth I stormed before her troops at Tilbury. She girded up her ruffs and challenged the Spanish ships: "I know I have the body of a weak and feeble woman, but I have the heart and stomach of a king, and a king of England too . . . "

Considering how she endured the beheading of her mother, the pox, prayer book revision, Calvinists, pirates, the Spider King, Pius V and toothache, she does indeed come across as more than a tripping Faerie Queene. In her carefully charted Ptolemaic cosmology, everything had a place and since God had chosen her to lead the cosmic dance she kept the time as soldiers and ships in an English universe paced their epicycles around her. It was the purposeful divine order and could give a woman the heart and stomach of a king. She believed that and it worked.

Still she was a woman and whether they watched her in council or on her deathbed, her ministers knew that was what made her. Before her brand of Leviathan was ever explained by Hobbes as eminently practical, she flaunted it as a sensual Occidental star. Once when she looked at the first woman to be married to an archbishop, the monarch in her affected an air of wounded noblesse but it took the woman in her to put it into words: " 'Madam' I may not call you; 'mistress' I am ashamed to call you; and so I know not what to call you."

Elizabeth was not present at the democratic General Convention of the Episcopal Church in 1970. That was good because next to monarchs, presidents and committees can look very drab; but it also was unfortunate because there was no one to enliven their speech. A woman at Convention made the drabbest speech of all. Explaining why she wanted to be ordained to the priesthood, she said that "in the Church, ordination is the mark of the professional."[1] When one gives up monarchs one has to make do with presidents; that is one thing. But when one gives up Catholicism one has to make do with professionals and that is more serious. The woman at Convention had made for herself a nasty bedfellow, the hoary old scarlet ultramontanist because she could not tell the difference between honest sacerdotalism and tired clericalism.

Elizabeth in her age could be as anti-clerical as a Lollard but she was a thorough sacerdotalist, unlike the later Victoria who thought the chief work of a clergyman was to ride and weep well. If she seems unreal to us it is because we have grown accustomed to thinking artificially of history; we belong to an age which confuses Henry VIII with Charles Laughton and believes Bette Davis engineered the Elizabethan Compromise. No such thing. Henry was a real man who died a Catholic and Elizabeth was a real woman who believed in the priesthood. Her plans disrupted clerical strategems but never the work of the altar. Sometimes she had to remind the priests of that work: "To your text, Mr. Dean! To your text!" One imagines Elizabeth hearing the woman at Convention call ordination "the mark of the professional" and, as the only monarch in a council of presidents, finding the statement not only theologically void but too bourgeois for words. Her reply, as one woman to another, would be familiar: ". . . I know not what to call you . . ."

* * *

No case for or against the ordination of women to the priesthood should be based on the merits of professionalism or clerical pragmatism. Theologically, these blow neither one way nor the other. What we are after is truth, not convenience. The great difficulty for us today is that we do not believe there is a difference. There usually is. The reader may tap the page at this point and say, "Ha! The Protestant Ethic." Or perhaps he will call it the masochistic line of a Madrid *penitente.* It is wonderful how ecumenical we can be when we find something we commonly dislike. None of this gets to the point. The point is honesty. Just because something works does not mean it is right. A fire may keep us warm but what if the logs are from the neighbor's woodpile? Samuel Butler, writing in the seventeenth century, considered the same problem with candescent cynicism:

> What makes all doctrines plain and clear?
> About two hundred pounds a year.
> And that which was prov'd true before,
> Prove false again? Two hundred more.[2]

As long as the priesthood is considered a mandarin class organized for bureaucratic utility, we easily bargain away any understanding of its supernatural integrity. Nearly twenty years ago, Kathleen Bliss asked in her book *The Service and Status of Women in the Churches,* why the Christian "ministry" should be "only or almost the only profession barred to women on the grounds of their sex."[3] First of all, she made a clear example of the confusion between ministry and priesthood in the minds of many supporters of the ordination of women. The obvious answer to her question is that the ministry is not barred to women; certainly that was manifested at the foot of the Cross and was "professionalized," if you will, at Cenchrea according to Romans and quite more widely according to I Timothy.[4] It was well underway when women began padding about Pachomian villages and was unmistakable when their Celtic counterparts assisted the carriage of the Sacrament from the village altar to neighboring homes. Remember the sturdy phrase of Pope Pius XI that men and woman are, together, "ministers, as it were, of the divine omnipotence."[5]

The ordained priesthood is a specific ministry barred to women and is not a necessary mark of the Christian ministry which is, in fact, only professional by virtue of our baptismal profession. To see the priesthood as a bureaucratic office and the priest as only a privileged clerk betrays our latent affection for the categories of the secular establishment against which we sometimes superficially protest. Unless the Church stops talking about its executives and professionals and pays more attention to its ministries, it will have nothing much to say to the world. Thomas Merton wrote:

> The real idols of our time are not religious, they are secular, and the real challenge to Christianity today is not a matter of mere Self-criticism and adaptation to the world, but above all the recovery of a creative and prophetic iconoclasm over against the idols of power, mystification and super-control. These tighten upon man and enclose him in a new world of mystery where the myths are no longer religious and spiritual but historical, political and pseudoscientific.[6]

The Church is used to hard things but the most painful one at the moment may be that we are breeding in this iron age people who, despite their baptism, get romantic about these new vernacular myths. That is what provokes the hauteur of *regina scientarum*.

None of this will make sense to the man who cannot see that the Church is different from the world. He may be the first one to speak of prophecy and the prophetic ministry but he will not consent to a secularly unacceptable language for the Church. He will ask for a logical statement about the priesthood without the slightest consideration that the supernature of the priesthood may surpass his natural vocabulary. He is in fact making an illogical request. Since the priesthood lays no claim to logical invention, any deep encounter with it must pass the province of natural religion.

William Law wrote of a character named Mundanus: "Mundanus aims at the greatest perfection in everything. The soundness and strength of his mind and his just way of thinking upon things make him intent upon removing all imperfections."[7] Mundanus would not for a moment be able to see the priesthood as something perfect. For example, to be perfect it must be just, and yet it excludes women. When a woman speaks of her right to the priesthood, Mundanus must summon his soundness and strength and his mind and his just way of thinking to her defence. Mundanus would be perfectly confounded at the suggestion that no one has a "right" to be ordained. It is not a democratic office, just as Christus Rex is not Christus Prexy. Take away His sceptre and give Him a Bill of Rights neatly tied with ribbon and you have the Christ of the Republican Way, the cosmic Christ constitutionalized.

Rather, ordinal procedure is a matter of vocation and acceptance by the Church in the name of Christ. That is why a bishop may quite arbitrarily deny the priesthood to any man, and it also is why in times past some bishops tied unwilling men hand and foot to ordain them. In our discussion we shall try to see why the "right" to be a priest belongs to the category of the right to be tall or musical. If all this affronts your sense of the sensible and fair American play, you are on the right track.

* * *

One of Anglicanism's great apologists cites a passage from *Pride and Prejudice:*

> "I should like Balls infinitely better," said Caroline Bingley, "if they were carried on in a different manner ... It would surely be much more rational if conversation instead of dancing made the order of the day." "Much more rational, I dare say," replied her brother, "but it would not be near so much like a Ball."[8]

C. S. Lewis then goes on to say that those who want women to be priestesses are sincere and pious and sensible, indeed too sensible. They play Caroline Bingley while truth must be the brother because the ordination of priestesses would make us much more rational "but not near so much like a Church." "The Church claims to be the bearer of a revelation. If that claim is false then we want not to make priestesses but to abolish priests."

If we were perfectly rational creatures, the way the world orders rationality, we should hardly be the image of God. Perfectly rational creatures are not men and women who live in community and fall in love, they are citizens of a state who have sex. "As the state grows more like a hive or an ant hill," Lewis observes, "it needs an increasing number of workers who can be treated as neuters."[9] Adam and Eve, Christ and the Church, have no place in such a world and in its building they must be crushed.

The alternative to the Orwellian nightmare is the right thought of Christ about sex but that has long seemed to most of us, as the truth is known, a neurotically repressive thing. Attempts to change that impression are usually made in an equally neurotic way by jejune clergymen overcompensating for lost delights by abolishing sin and shouting eureka about it all like some latter-day Archimedes leaping up with his trousers down.

The United States, and its clergy, can hardly do justice to the full implications of Christian sensuality since they have never come face to face with historic Catholicism. The principal type of Catholicism in this country has been Roman Catholicism of the Irish variety and that hybrid of old line Jansenism is so essentially Calvinist that it quickly made its capital Boston. Jansenism was a peculiar Continental form of pietism which agreed with the line in the film "The African Queen" that nature is something we are put on earth to overcome.

American Catholicism would be quite as befuddled as American Protestantism to hear D.H. Lawrence lauding sensuality as essentially the gift of Catholicism's sight of the cosmic mystery while denoucing secularism as the sterilizing enemy of the sexes: "We are bleeding at the roots, because we are cut off from the earth and sun and stars and love is a grinning mockery, because, poor blossom, we plucked it from its stem on the tree of life, and expected it to keep on blooming in our civilized vase on the table."[10]

* * *

While the matter itself is profoundly theological, there is no burning theological issue initiating the discussion of women in Holy Orders. The inspiration is basically utilitarian. There are those who claim theological motives for altering what they claim is but a secular obstacle. The real situation is quite the opposite: secular considerations demand the alteration of theological obstacles. They say there is no supernatural argument against priestesses, only natural, and that, we are made to realize is apparently what they have been put on earth to overcome. In reality, as long as the priesthood is the priesthood of Christ, no words about it can be "only" natural. The sentence to the Colossians should haunt us: "Be on your guard; do not let your minds be captured by hollow and devisive speculations, based on traditions of man-made teaching and centered on the elemental spirits of the world and not on Christ."[11]

All this debate comes at a time when women are finally achieving many of their right and proper claims to a full share of the professional and economic markets. Inasmuch as an attitude prevails which is conditioned by generations of church establishment, parties concerned will see nothing irregular in applying to the priesthood the secular imperative of "rights."

This is all part, perhaps, of the strange circular course of history: when a person attempting modern reform establishes an equation between Holy Orders and professions he is in fact marked with the company of bewigged Erastians in the eighteenth century and later. The 1958 regulation for ordaining women in the Swedish State Church, for instance, is part and parcel with the Hanoverian manipulation of bishoprics which finally led to John Keble's Assize Sermon on National Apostasy in 1833. The Swedish regulation was fundamentally determined not by theological directions but by the requirement of equal opportunity in civil offices, just as the British Government's decision to suppress certain Irish bishoprics in 1833 was entirely a matter of civil expediency. Keble had to tell the judges of the courts that bishops are not mandarins but apostles. That kind of prophecy has been muted in our generation. When the priesthood is plucked by secular hands to blossom in a civilized vase it truly is a grinning mockery.

Chapter II

NEITHER MALE NOR FEMALE

We make a dangerous distinction between our epistemological faculties when we say that there are no theological arguments against the ordination of women, but only psychological ones. To begin with, never since Freud took up his pen have we been able to use the phrase "only psychological!" What is psychologically pertinent for the Christian must also be theologically pertinent.

The contemporary abhorrence of the word "priestess" is an example of psychological opposition; to try and solve the problem by adjusting the term is like the game of sweeping the conflict between "minister" and "priest" under a rug called "presbyter," an illicit tidiness found even in men like Richard Hooker. Unlike the Latin *sacerdos* and the Greek *hiereus,* there is nothing epicene about the English *priest;* it has a female counterpart, priestess, and to say "woman priest" is semantically as adroit as saying "female rooster."

One psychological concomitant of the use of "priestess" is that it knocks the pride of contemporaneity out of us. "Priestess" is not a new term and its use does not make us fashionably *moderne* however much we pretend. It is probably older than "priest." The title of an article on the ordination of women in a recent publication of the Episcopal Church read "Right On into the Twentieth Century."[1] What is particularly space age about priestesses is obscure; insofar as their western European and Mesopotamian precedents alike refer us to sybilline declamations over animals innards, they are foremostly archeological.

The burden of the archeology, however, is that eventually we uncover an identity with the past which is as real theologically as ceremonially. To be specific, the great danger of our new enterprise is that when we say sex is unimportant in determining who should be in the priesthood we are in effect making a very ancient and heretical statement common to the early Docetists, Manicheans and related Gnostics that matters of the spirit are debased by association with sex. This is a psychophysical dualism opposing soul and body and is completely contrary to the Christian way, as well as to most modern analysis.

It is too easy for one travelling in the sphere of theology to forget that in order to reach the proper destination one must travel on the side of the road not customary in our own country. As we in 1971 decide to rush headlong into the Twentieth Century our excitement leads us into the lane approved by the secular traffic and that is going the wrong way. Consequently, if we appear to ourselves to have become psychedelic, it is only because we have regressed to the Gnostic world of ca.250 where Manes and his cultic vegetarians are clad in red and blue mantles, juggling silver stars and, in the eyes of God, looking rather silly.

* * *

One of the things we must tolerate in order to be breathing Christians is that sexual difference is one of the special gifts, charismata, of God. God did not make a woman because he was too short on ribs for another man. Adam was pleased, too pleased, with the new creation; the problem in the Garden was not that God made Eve inferior to Adam, but that Adam made his wife superior to God. The price they both paid for that action was the fruit which turned them into theologians, theologians in rank with those heretical dualists who were offended by the carnal part of the Incarnate God and who, along with their blood-brothers in the Twentieth Century, were violated by Peter's witness that flesh as well as spirit had emptied the Easter tomb. God's crudeness in giving Adam and Eve sexes shocked their newly wise spirituality so they proceeded to dress themselves in the academic robes of the world's first Docetists: Figleaves.

> They who believe
> Their bodies are *not* loosed from death, do not
> Believe the Lord, who wills to raise His own
> Works sunken; or else say they that the Good
> Wills not, and that the Potent hath not power,
> Ignorant from how great a crime they suck
> Their milk, in daring to set things infirm
> Above the Strong.[2]

* * *

Anthropologically, it would seem that priestesses have been common, not in orthodox Jewish and Christian cultures which acknowledge the merits of Eden before the Fall, but rather in those which have been either decidedly matriarchal or decidedly contemptuous of women. The affinity between them is that the privileged uniqueness of the sexes is for neither a divine preoccupation. Since the former is probably limited to Amazonia and the United States, the truth of this is more evident in the lands of the male jingoists.

Hellenic culture, for example, permitted priestesses alongside a canonized contempt for female liberty. At the time men and women were travelling together along the Palestinian byways with Jesus, we are told that Hellenistic domestic conditions had changed very little since the time Xenophon wrote the Oikonomikos. The woman functioned as a sacrificing machine in the temples and a reproductive machine in the houses. Romance was carried on without women. Yet this was a culture which maintained priestesses with disarming readiness. Likewise, in 1952 when Japan hardly symbolized a place of sexual equality, the United Church of Christ (the Kyodan) was pioneering in the ordination of women, counting over a hundred female ministers among its clergy.[3] As long as women are utilitarian chattel, they will be to a religion what vassals were to a feudal lord. Simone de Beauvoir, in her charter of female liberty, described the fief condition:

> Man has succeeded in enslaving woman; but in the same degree he has deprived her of what made her possession desirable. With woman integrated in the family and society, her magic is dissipated rather than transformed; reduced to the condition of servant, she is no longer that unconquered prey incarnating all the treasures of nature.[4]

If woman's only worth is her practical usefulness, she will be permitted to do whatever religion practically requires. If, on the other hand, we have a Church which could practically use priestesses but refuses for theological reasons then we have found a Church awed by the proposition that a woman is nothing less than a woman. Denial can be the highest deference.

* * *

In the good news of Christianity is the equality of the sexes. This shocks both the male and female bigot who confuse equality with sameness. It is not that way at all. Indeed, the basic requirement for things to be equal is that they be different. The government does not assure me of equality with myself, but with different men of creation. We do not demonstrate so that whites and whites will be treated equally in the courts. Equality is a term of difference.

Secularly, the ideal of human equality has rarely succeeded and that is partially so because of the absence of a divine reference. Political pragmatism or secular humanism does not bear the burden of human passion. What is needed is something more than a human type to represent the genius of equality. Without this, the vision becomes distorted, equality means sameness and there is no escape. Either one buys that conformity or he does not and the tragedy is that it does not make one bit of difference. When persons and societies are denied the vision of equality as freedom they share a common myopia, regardless of politics, and are blind to any real option. Study the gray ranks of machined men chanting in Peking Square about communal glory and the files of Western men in their metropolitan tabernacles dryly hymning a God who ordered "the rich man in his castle, the poor man at his gate." Equality as freedom is a dead word in both worlds. By no mere coincidence is the gray flannel suit the common uniform of Peking and Madison Avenue.

The consequences of this malaise are evident in secular manipulation of the sexes. The two pronounced reactions to the reality of maleness and femaleness are obliteration and exploitation. Obliteration is having its radical moment in our time; exploitation is historic. Obliteration belongs to the school which identifies equality with sameness; exploitation is the manner of those who either for cultural or private psychological reasons panic at the implications of that illicit identification.

The weight of human prejudice and jealousy is too great for man to assert sexual equality or any other kind of equality alone. The first truths held to be self-evident in the Declaration of Independence are that all men are created equal and that they are endowed by the Creator with certain inalienable rights. This is a matter of religion; any talk of equality is always religious. To make the religious statement secure there must be the assurance of divine assent. Even the French National Assembly in 1789 was compelled to declare the Rights of Man and of the Citizen "under the auspices of the Supreme Being." When people think they have discovered a profundity by observing that all men are *not* created equal because some are clever and others are not or because some are musical and others are not, they are ignoring the theology of equality and are rather skimming the surface for the indigestible cream that says equality is a purely utilitarian matter of interchangeability. They suggest to us that Thomas Jefferson was speaking not of men but of chameleons.

For these reasons, the United Nation's Universal Declaration of Human Rights, while a lofty document and far more exhaustive than the Delcaration of Independence, is a fundamental failure. It is entirely based on secular suppositions. The justifying preamble contains seven clauses which are perfectly correct as far as they go but there is no reference to a qualifying authority. The first clause reads. "Whereas recognition of the inherent dignity and of the equal and inalienable rights of all members of the human family is the foundation of freedom, justice and peace in the world . . . " The response of common sense must be, "Says who?" and when the answer comes back, "The General Assembly of the United Nations on December 10, 1948," anyone who disagrees can go back to shooting up a jungle or violating a border with perfect serenity. Of course, he will most likely do the same thing if we credit the authority to God but at least we will not be playing the man for a fool.

To Jacques Maritain it seemed that for such an enormous thing as equality, a *deus ex machina* is in order. Structures for the organization of men based on equality of being cannot be justified by popular action because then they can be denied by popular action. Classically, Julius Caesar has collapsed on Shakespearean stages over and over again to prove what Crassus and Pompey already found out, that non-Trinitarians cannot apotheosize a triumvirate. Triumvirates and troikas, the perfect microcosm of collective equality, must always fail if they have no justifying reference beyond a common agreement that they are convenient.

The Christian, however, has a divine authority for equality, a triumvirate that does not fail and this has implications for the specific matter of sexual equality. In the Trinity, the Father, the Son and the Holy Spirit are absolutely one in their existence, and yet that existence operates in three different manifestations, all three of which are equal in dignity and being. This society of the Trinity is the light that makes sense of the co-existent equality and difference in human maleness and femaleness. Just as the persons of the Trinity express divinity in different ways, so are these sexual realities distinct manifestations of humanity while being absolutely one in their humanity, common in both dignity and being.

* * *

In all honest Christian theology, statements initially are experiences rather than ideas. The dictum is true that ours is a metaphysic based on a religion and not the other way around. Never, of course, does this sanction the sort of "gut-thinking" which has its current advocates; it is not the emotionalism of Matthew Arnold's assertion, "Only what we feel, we know."[5] It is simply a statement that supernatural truths come to us by divine design and active encounter with the world around us and not solely by private mental initiative. If the latter were the case, each of us should be teetering on the brink of solipsism, seeing in our individual vision the measure and reality of everything.

Consequently, we must recognize, contrary to much cushioned thinking of the last few years, that the Trinity was objectively revealed to men in historical encounters and is the fundamental reference for all historic activity. It did not first lighten upon the world as a private amusement for scholars during intermissions at Nicaea nor was it a sublimation of one of Athanasius's choleric attacks. True enough, this mystery which is "above reason but not against it" as it made itself real in experience seems implicit rather than explicit in most of the New Testament. One Pauline scholar, for example, says of his subject: "The three coordinate Beings of the Athanasian creed and of so much popular thought, Beings standing in a relation of absolute equality in which, except for the phrases about generation and procession there is 'no before or after,' this for him would have been incomprehensible." But uncanny evidence of an understanding of relationships of Beings is given in the style of many of his analogies and we may particularly see his description of the relationship between men and women as proof of his sensitivity to what must be going on in the commerce of the Trinity. Such existential witness as this gave the fire to kindle later patristic and conciliar thought.6

See, as an example, the part in I Corinthians in which he wants us to know "that Christ is the head of every individual man, just as a man is the 'head' of the woman and God is the head of Christ." Then, in practically the same breath, he reminds his Corinthian friends, "Of course, in the sight of God neither 'man' nor 'woman' has any separate existence. For if woman was made originally for man, no man is now born except by a woman, and both man and woman, like everything else, owe their existence to God."7

This is the majesty of the Divine reference, but the perfection of this system of distinction side by side with free equality is apparent only to the Trinitarian believer. The distinction between woman and man is a recognition of being and not of dignity; it is no more a mark of inferiority than is the distinction between Christ and the Father — man is the head of the woman and God, meaning the Father, is the head of Christ. It is the most natural consistency among supernatural realities and explains at least part of that mysterious idea that the Three in One made man and woman in his own image. "In the image of God created he them." (On the other hand, since he has rejected subordination between the persons of the Trinity only he can understand why subordination between the sexes which are in the image of God is more than injustice, it is heresy.) On this point we must part company with Athanasius who defended subordination in the Trinity and Aquinas who used subordination in the sexes as a reason for barring women from the priesthood.

This discrimination, then, has no argument against equality or freedom. It is the order which secures the possiblity of equality and freedom and as such is a divine gift. So Karl Rahner writes:

> All order and structure must be thought of as an inner moment within freedom, as one of freedom's intrinsic elements: they cannot be in ultimate opposition. This is the only

way in which the affirmation of freedom does not lead to a position of atheism. This is the only way in which God can be seen as the absolutely unique and primordial origin both of freedom *and* of structure and order together.[8]

* * *

One of the most disreputable tacks in the discussion involves the citation of St. Paul's great statement in his letter to the Galatians, "there is neither male nor female: for you are all one in Christ Jesus" as a qualification for ordaining women to the priesthood.[9] That is classical reductionism. He is not clapping his hands to announce a genetic revolution. "Neither male nor female" is no more a statement of natural biology or psychology than "neither bond nor free" is sociology or "neither Jew nor Greek" is anthropology. In the same sense, when we sing "In Christ there is no east or west," we do not mean to find pagodas in Sioux City.

St. Paul is speaking a heavenly language, declaring what can only be an apocaplyptic verity and, even in that case, the "homoousion" of man and woman says nothing against the reality of men and women just as the "homoousion" of the Father and the Son does not deny that Jesus prayed to His Father and now sits at His right hand. The prayer of Christ is, "That they all may be one; as thou Father, art in me, and I in thee, that they also may be one in us."[10]

For the terrestrial moment the Church must be sacramental enough to perceive the present realities of sex, status and culture, exalting that which is good in each and castigating that which is insulting both to God and to us. Secular exploitation of sexual differences in fields which theoretically have no sexual restrictions violate the Christian mind but that is a far different matter from the divine discrimination which merely states the reality of different sexes. St. Paul's statement about male and female eradicates the fact of maleness and femaleness no more than his statement about bond and free or Jew and Greek denies the reality of Onesimus and Philemon or the fundamentals of geography. Certainly his readers know this; that is the source of one of the great ironies of the ordinal controvery: proponents of priestesses quickly label St. Paul an anti-feminist on the grounds of his abiding awareness of the different order of men and women yet they simultaneously use his own writing in Galatians 3:28 as a proof text for the indistinguishability which he himself found so grim. Having sighted the careful line between representation and misrepresentation, these exegetes have approached it with all the temerity of Caesar at the Rubicon.

Chapter III

MUD AND DIAMONDS

If one wishes to get anywhere in understanding the choices Christ made in choosing sacramental signs, one must continue to escape the semantic confinement of thinking that discrimination is a sin. It is the way we get on in a world of light and dark. Pity the indiscriminate soul. Right discrimination is an acknowledgement of the freedom to choose between right and wrong. It is proof that long ago we bit into the fruit and found out that good and bad have names. Anything less is fantasy of the sort imagined by W. H. Auden's Simeon:

> As long as the apple had not been entirely digested,
> As long as there remained the least understanding
> between Adam and the stars, rivers and horses with
> whom he had once known complete intimacy, as long as
> Eve could share in any way with the moods of the
> rose or the ambitions of the swallow, there was still
> a hope that the effects of the poison would wear off,
> that the exile from Paradise was only a bad dream,
> that the Fall had not occurred in fact.[1]

The moment we feel within ourselves the parallelism between right and wrong on the one hand and good and evil on the other, we intuitively affirm a prime canon of Kantian aesthetics: the beauty of an object is determined by the degree to which it approximates its purpose.[2] In moral terms, the degree to which something is good is the degree to which it is "right" for its role. This is a matter of sensible discrimination. So, for instance, Socrates is quoted by Xenophon as saying that if the one be beautifully fitted to its purpose and the other ill, "a dung-basket may be beautiful and a gold shield ugly."[3] St.

Augustine followed suit by asking, "What is the value of a golden key if it does not open the door I wish to enter, or what is the harm of a wooden one if it does?"[4] A beautiful political speech is essentially ugly if delivered to Londoners in Ugric; assuming that the omnicompetence of the British fails when it comes to the tongue of the Ugrian, the speech must fail in its purpose to convince. It becomes like the shield or the golden key.

Christ seems to have acted on this principle in his choice of signs. Now we may assume that His choice of bread and wine for the Eucharistic meal or His choice of water for baptismal washing was arbitrary; he could have used lamb and cider in the Upper Room or crackers and Coca Cola if we prefer it that way and He could have rolled in the mud on the bank of the Jordan or sprinkled Himself with diamonds but He chose to discriminate. There is nothing innately supernatural about these forms. But their symbolism effectively aids the accomplishment of the objective purposes of grace: they adequately serve the traditional types used in Hebraic Scripture and help make earthly sense of an unearthly action. Water gives life, bread sustains it and wine makes it glad. Inasmuch as these signs are right for their purpose, as Our Lord's discrimination acknowledged, they are good. Substitutes, then, are rejected not for pedantic reasons but because they are aeshtetically wrong and hence bad.

Just as Christ discriminated in choosing bread and wine and not lamb and cider and water and not mud or diamonds, so He discriminated in choosing men and not women for the apostolic function of His ordered priesthood. We shall later consider the merits of this symbolic function. For the moment it remains that it was a significance sufficiently obvious to the High Priest Himself. It was also rigid enough to prohibit the inclusion of any of the many women about Him. Was the avoidance of women not by design but rather conditioned by a cultural provincialism? There are a great many who say yes. The record, however, is clear that Christ took no cultural norm for granted; after all, He stormed the Temple and broke some of the most carefully guarded laws in the Book. "He discarded the cosmic powers and authorities like a garment."[5] If the argument stands that Christ was only acquiescing to unjust public custom with regard to women, He is not the Perfect Man but a perfect hypocrite and is certainly not Emmanuel.[6]

Aesthetically and morally, priestesses as substitutes for priests turn wrong or bad in the manner of cider or mud or diamonds. In the safe assumption that Christ realized the full right and wrong of things we can say this: as with the other sacramental signs, there is nothing innately more righteous about a man than a woman, indeed one might ordinarily make an easy case for the opposite. Nevertheless, in the mysterious symbolism understood by God "he" and not "she" as an analogy of Christ before the congregation of the faithful seemed "right" and therefore "good." The practice of priestesses, then, remains more than aesthetically inappropriate or ugly, it is morally bad.

When we wonder at psychological objections to the idea of priestesses, one may say that we are reacting aesthetically rather than theologically but, and this is the crux of it all, the aesthetic statement is essentially theological. Psychological aversion to a woman "dressed as a priest" or calling herself a priest is more than a fickle bias. We would not call a person fickle if he objected to a beard on Botticelli's Venus. Inappropriateness is ugliness and ugliness is bad; only Screwtape denies that a Dionysius rattles his drums. One thing is certain: the recent position of the National Organization of Women which maintained that the discrimination against women in the ordinal canons implies inferiority is a heady dose of sophistry. In light of the fact that Divine discrimination in choosing men and women for the priesthood is as definite as the determinations of genetics, men might as well complain that they are denied childbearing.

In his classic work on the *Ministerial Priesthood* Dr. Moberly wrote:

> If God is not in any way bound to His own appointed methods of grace, yet we are. Outside his appointed "media" of whatever kind — ministries, sacraments, ordinances — He can work, if He will, as divinely as within them. He can cleanse with Abana, or with Pharpar, or with nothing, as effectively as with Jordan. But that is nothing to us, if He has bidden us to wash in Jordan.7

Any argument which dismisses discrimination on the basis of function, whether practical as with golden keys and shields or priests, or symbolic as with the sacramental signs and the priesthood, cannot disregard the glaring discrimination in another sacrament: Holy Matrimony. The logical extension of the position of the National Organization of Women on the matter of Holy Orders should be an objection to the sexual discrimination in the marriage canons which specify that one party be male and one be female. Why not two men or two women? We have already pointed out the latent Docetism in much of the pro-priestess material. If that position is to be systematic at all, we must be prepared to trip back to happy Hellenism in more ways than one.

With all laud to what William Cowper called "the sex whose presence civilizes ours," when it comes to the institution of the Christian priesthood we must freely adapt William Butler: "Doubtless God could have made a better berry, but doubtless God never did."

Chapter IV

OUR MOTHER WHO ART IN HEAVEN

In the ancient Greek world, gods and goddesses had their spirited moments, trysting in the spheres of human converse, giving men a glimpse of divinity come out of the clouds. This interest in things divine, things beyond men and controlling men, was narcissistic rather than transcendent; it was in actuality a quest of the superhuman rather than the supernatural; there was little telling between the two. The inhabitants of the Olympian firmament, whether Bacchus with his capacity for wine or Aeolus with his capacity for wind, were mightier than men.

Since this was a rationnal pantheon, empiricism writ large (even the gods at their sublimest knew the inhibitions of natural law, getting drunk or tired), reform came only when the intellect felt itself being vulgarized as when Plato banned Homeric tales from being told in his ideal Republic. Aestheticism, because it plucked the tautest chord and highest note of the intellectual vision, defined the mystical experience for the Greeks. Here lay the error next to the splendor. Beauty became sublimity itself rather than a means to the sublime which is God. Consequently ugliness became evil itself rather than its description. God is beautiful. The Greeks, however, said beauty is God and that is quite a different matter; just as people today take the mighty phrase "God is love" and reduce it to sentimental atheism by saying "love is God."

The problem is that when you become so cerebral, and consequently sentimental since sentimentality is the co-heir of superficial intellectualism and ignorance, practical things like people become an embarrassment. They may readily buy the idea that love is God, for instance, but when they find that goosebumps do not much help the man who is alone or Grandfather on his deathbed, they will curse that they were not given God at all but rather a romantic enchantment. Only then do they discover how hard a spell can be to undo. So also when the Greeks had idealized beauty until it became God, the common lot found that the price they had to pay was the glory of their own bodies "warts and all." Perfection could not abide differences; there was an intellectual ideal which shunned even the sexuality of the old gods and required that the natural body had to be "improved" just as the Victorians "improved" old country Gothic churches. The Greeks would have considered the realistic characterization of Roman portraiture decadent. Serenity rather than passion set the tone of divinity. The Hermaphrodite was apotheosized. In his brilliant study of the Renaissance, Walter Pater noticed how "the beauty of the gods had the least traces of sex. Here, there is a moral sexlessness, a kind of ineffectual wholeness of nature, yet with a higher beauty and insignificance of its own."[1]

That is, to paraphrase an earlier observation, "much more rational" than the art of the Church but not at all like the Christian God who sweat naked in His manhood before His mother. That is precisely why the Greeks found Christ foolish. Impassiblity in the formal sense of the Greek *Apatheia* is far removed from God as revealed to the Church, because impassibility in the Christian vocabulary only means that God is not subject to the actions of any other being; the world hung in a balance for three dark days until Easter announced that. Impassibility in the Christian scheme does not prevent God from involving Himself in wordly affairs in a way we would call, in our language, passionate to the point of death. And yet that passion does not mitigate the fact that His plans do not change and that He is always God:

> When Israel was a child, then I loved him and
>   called my son out of Egypt.
> As they called them, so they went from them:

> they sacrificed unto Baalim and burned
> incense to graven images.
> I taught Ephraim also to go, taking them by
> their arms; but they knew not that I healed
> them.
> I drew them with cords of a man, with bands of
> love: and yet I was to them as they that
> take off the yoke on their jaws, and I
> laid meat unto them . . .
> How shall I give thee up, Ephraim? How shall
> I deliver thee, Israel? How shall I make
> thee as Admah? How shall I set thee as
> Zeboim? My heart is turned within me, my
> repentings are kindled together.
> I will not execute the fierceness of mine anger,
> I will not return to destroy Ephraim: for I
> am God and not man; the Holy One in the
> midst of thee: and I will not enter into
> the city.[2]

Gifted as we are with the facts of revelation, we can no longer dapple ourselves in the quiet serenity of superhuman perfection. Our God is not an "it", for neuters do not love and call us out of Egypt. Nor does the transcendence of this God who is "not man" make His maleness interchangeable with femaleness; that would be superhuman but it would not be supernatural. What is the full measure of God we do not know, but He has loved us and taught us to call Him Father.

* * *

If a Christian rejects revelation and makes himself indifferent to sexual language for God, he may change the lesson given by Christ to the disciples who asked how to pray and instead pray, "Our Mother which art in heaven." That avoids the Deism inherent in prayers to a Supreme Being but it is theologically traumatic. While it may be maintained that the motherhood of God is a half-truth in that He gives character and birth and nurture to creation, it is also a half-lie which the Fatherhood of God is not. God established His freedom to be with us as perfect God in a totally masculine nature while no revelation has ever displayed His freedom to so exist in an expressly feminine way. On the contrary, the Incarnation gave a total affirmation of the difference of men from women and the difference of Christ from the perfect woman. The difference was marked at Cana with the words, "Woman, what have I to do with thee?" and was sealed with the words from the cross, "Woman, behold thy son."[3] Because of these things we may say that any prayer to God beginning "Our Mother which art in heaven" is a misaddress because the entire corpus of Catholic theology has maintained that the mother in Heaven is Mary.

Those who see no obstacle to ordaining priestesses are quite generally of a school which has little sympathy with Mariology. That explains in part their confusion and their ready assumption that Catholic practice is anti-feminist. Just the opposite, that epithet can only be given most unadvisedly to that tradition which has venerated a woman as the Prime Human of the race and which has, sometimes with astonishing nonchalance, given women rule over countless priests and people. Hilda of Whitby and Theresa of Avila were no lackies. Instead, we must realize that the gravest anti-feminist crime in the history of Christendom was the alienation of the Virgin Mary from hyperdulia in the aftermath of the Reformers, grinding to dust the Marian praises of Luther himself.

Mary is the figurehead of the human race and, specifically, of the Church. Totally human, she knew the smell of stables next to the cedarwood and incense of the Temple. She differs from Christ in that she is solely human; her speech and actions are not a mediation between men and God but are offered up as the full response of the human race to the Creator. She is the Perfect Woman and not what certain schools of witchcraft called her, the Anomalous Woman. It was to assure the Christian people of this that St. Thomas Aquinas and St. Bernard among others strongly opposed any formulation of her immaculate conception.

As human and not divine, it is the case that her role in the economy of salvation was not preordained as was Christ's. The whole possibility of reconciling man and God hung in the balance until she agreed to let God have his way and then sang the Magnificat, bringing to a radical conclusion in her radical experience the song of Miriam who sang the exodus and the song of Deborah who sang the victory of Israel. In the drama of her song all women and, more truthfully, the whole human race were given a dignity beyond our daring: the eternal Father would not act until a human voice said Yes. So the consummation of the Divine Marriage proceeded and the Church has always been styled as feminine along with all creation because it freely responded to a powerful Will which burned to fill it with new life. Obdurate and vulgar are persons who charge that the Annunciation is a perfect example of a woman being used.

E. L. Mascall has given us this understanding:

> "It was *male human nature* the Son of God united to His divine person; it was a *female human person* who was chosen to be His mother. On the other hand, no *male human person* was chosen to be the Messiah. (To suppose so was the error of the adoptionists), and *no female human nature* was assumed by a divine person. Thus from one point of view the Incarnation exalts the male above the female while from another point of view it exalts the female sex above the male. In no woman has *human nature* been raised to the dignity which it possesses in Jesus of Nazareth, but in no male human person has there been given the dignity comparable to that which Mary enjoys as the Mother of God . . ."[4]

Dr. E. O. James, a priest and anthropologist, adds that science has, if anything, enhanced the role of Mary by debunking Aristotelian biology which gave the mother a purely receptive role in procreation; most probably, "the whole of Christ's human genetic inheritance was derived from Mary."[5] In the young Jewish girl, probably teenaged, God and the human race walked hand in hand more than any pagan could imagine.

Call her the mythical shadow of some Nile goddess or Greek sea legend, she will spitelessly continue her intercessions for us, confounding our embarrassment at the scandalous ways of God.

The case cannot rest without pointing out that one early Christian sect which had no qualms about giving deaconesses powers so great that the Council of Epaon in 517 had to limit the order was the Nestorian community which simultaneously denounced the promulgation of Mary as Theotokos, Mother of God. There is also significance in the fact that the one evidence of women bishops in self-styled early Christian churches was in certain Gnostic sects of Asia Minor which, in their ecstatic vision, rejected this orthodox understanding of the role of sex in nature, human and divine, and misread the Virgin as a condemnor of the flesh rather than a glorifier of its grace. Purity and puritanism are no more synonymous than alcohol and alcoholism. Mary's purity has a pulsing vigor, heightening the heady cymbal music of Exodus and Judges, putting down the pompous and sending the fat-cats away empty in order to exalt, not the impotent and neurotic, but the pure and the good.

Karl Barth says someplace, "Every time people want to fly from this miracle, a theology is at work, which has ceased to understand and honour the mystery as well... And on the other hand, where this mystery has been understood and men have avoided any attempt at natural theology, because they had no need of it, the miracle came to be thankfully and joyously recognized." How many times have we sung "Ye Watchers and ye Holy Ones" without the faintest glimmer that it was Mary of whom we sang when we came to the verses, "O Higher than the cherubim More glorious than the seraphim?" Call that our failure, it is also the ignorance of any person who says the Church denies the highest things to women.

Chapter V

REACHING A DECISION

Judging from Acts and the evidence of the pastoral letters of the New Testament, the roots of Catholic ordinal custom is pre-Nicene. Certainly, that has been a constant justification of the Anglican Church in her understanding of Holy Orders without a papacy and it was part of her defense when Leo XIII threw down the gauntlet against the validity of those orders in his 1896 letter "Apostolicae Curiae."[1]

Likewise, Catholic ordinal custom with respect to women is a classic example of tradition according to the canon delineated by St. Vincent of Lerins, *i.e.,* a practice of belief common to the Church "everywhere, to everyone, at all times." One commentator remarks that St. Vincent "would seem to allow for an organic development of doctrine analogous to the growth of the human body from infancy to age. But this development, he is careful to explain, while real, must not result in the least alteration to the original significance of the doctrine concerned. Thus in the end the Christian must, like Timothy (1 Timothy 6:20) 'guard the deposit,' that is, the revelation enshrined in its completeness in Holy Scripture and correctly interpreted in the Church's unerring tradition."[2]

It would surprise everyone in the procession from Richard Hooker to the Fathers of the Lambeth Quadrilateral of 1888 to hear that the Vincentian Canon is alien to Anglican tradition. What should be pointed out is that Anglicanism has often indicted the Roman Catholic Church for allegedly contravening the Canon. This is specifically the case with regard to papal infallibility, the Immaculate Conception, the Assumption and the Tridentine understanding of transubstantiation. In matters of organization it, of course, came to the fore in the Tudor break with the papacy, but that was long before anticipated in the Celtic sentiments which lost the day at the seventh century Synod of Whitby but continued in appeal to the minds of many English kings before Henry VIII. In a different interest it was also used as a defence of the episcopate against the Puritan claims of the seventeenth century, beginning with James I and the Hampton Court Conference in 1604.

Ordination of women is indeed a theological matter. Its accomplishment must involve a denial of our case against both papaism and presbyterianism: Catholic tradition firmly based on Scripture. It is genuinely hard to imagine how we might defend the validity of our ordinal tradition with the Latin and Eastern Churches or maintain any difference from the custom of the Reformed bodies were we to disassociate ourselves from Scriptural precedent and Catholic custom by ordaining women to preside at the Eucharist.

In a matter so portentous, only the decision of a truly ecumenical council can matter. That has been the attitude of Anglicanism with regard to such issues as universal canonization of saints and largely explains Anglican reluctance to establish machinery comparable to that in Rome for any such procedure; we maintain that universal acts require universal bodies and for that reason the promulgations of Rome and even of Vatican II are essentially provincial in weight. Speaking of priestesses, Dr. Macquarrie writes: "...one must wait for a development of a consensus on this matter within the Church as a whole, in all its major branches. It would be a divisive step for one diocese, one regional church, or even one communion, to act unilaterally in this matter."[3] Catholic Christendom, in the light of the reality of Anglicanism and Orthodoxy outside the obedience of Rome, is a Church divided and as such cannot be the complete voice of Pentecost.

The Anglican Communion has been careful to proceed upon precedent and that is not the same conservatism as that which once directed curates "never to do anything for the first time";

it merely requires authenticity for new things. Vernacular liturgies and married priests, for example, have recommended through the use of this standard. Insofar as they have Scriptural and traditional precedent, they are issues far removed form the ordination of priestesses. The Lambeth Conference has decided nothing which compromises the Vincentian Canon. Should it ever wish to do so, it could not anyway since its recommendations are only expressions of episcopal attitude and are in no way binding. Were it the belief of the Catholic bodies that the Holy Spirit willed the contravention of the norms of the pre-Nicene church as established by Scripture and tradition, they could properly proceed only through the convocation of a truly ecumenical council at least as comprehensive as a pan-Catholic Council of Jerusalem theoretically suggested by some Roman Catholic progressives in conference recently in Brussels.

The danger is that the exigencies of the moment and the prejudices of secularity may lead us to confuse Catholic conciliarism with meager bureaucracy . Are we to permit the idea that our Anglican councils have complete province in the matter? This obviously is where Churchmanship becomes important; and it is not the superficial thing we often take it for. The recent experience of Anglicanism in the ordinal controversy has shown an affinity between "Low Churchmen" and "High Churchmen." General opposition to priestesses at the Tenth Lambeth Conference in 1968, for instance, was largely shepherded by Marcus Loane, Archbishop of Sydney and a prime Evangelical. High and Low, and certainly not the latitudinarian belt in between, have historically had the greatest contests against the claims of both Rome and Geneva in whose shadows their Anglicanism might on occasion have seemed opaque. Both parties, claiming Catholic and Reformed truths, have had to make clear especially to uncritical minds how and why they continued as Anglicans. Both parties, therefore, have had reason especially to be jealous of Anglican claims to Scriptural and traditional authenticity. Their causes are too great and too widely challenged to risk the facile equipage of a vague reductionism.

> ... it seems obvious that what unite the Evangelical and the Anglo-Catholic against the "liberal" or "modernist" is something very clear and momentous, namely, the fact that both are thoroughgoing supernaturalists, who believe in the Creation, the Fall, the Incarnation, the Resurrection, the Second Coming and the Four Last Things. This unites them not only with one another, but with the Christian religion as understood *ubique et ab omnibus.*
>
> The point of view from which this agreement seems less important than their divisions, or than the gulf which separates both from any non-miraculous version of Christianity, is to me unintelligible. Perhaps the trouble is that as supernaturalists, whether "Low" or "High" Church, thus taken together, they lack a name. May I suggest "Deep Church"; or, if that fails in humility, Baxter's "Mere Christians"?[4]

Newman gave firm assent to this in his *Apologia:* "This is what the Church is said to want, not party men, but sensible, temperate, sober, well-judging persons, to guide it through the channel of no-meaning, between the Scylla and Charybdis of Aye and No."[5]

Such men are the prophets we need right now, and they will rarely be recognized because they are too radical for the radical; their hopes for a perfect home embarrass the utopian; their certitude is too brave for the guerilla; and their vision of humanity astonishes the humanitarian. They will write poetry in banks and fairy tales in the corners of pubs. Sometimes they will puff pipes and, like T. S. Eliot, call themselves classicists or monarchists or even Anglo-Catholics, bemused at the rage of their cultured despisers who claimed not be listening. In the end they will not be brightly martyred but, dressed in sack suits and cassocks, will slowly be tightened out of the human parliament for the crime of pronouncing glory instead of mere good.

Chapter VI

LAMBETH

Recent developments in the ordinal question at Lambeth consultations have brought the Anglican Communion to a reckoning with her historic understanding of the Church as the meeting of earthly and heavenly kingdoms. Never since Keble's Assize Sermon stirred the Tractarian reformers at Oxford, have so many men found themselves in the awkward and threatening position of defending Christian orthodoxy not against mischievous doctrinal heresy but against doctrinal apathy. It is a sweepingly prophetic posture. The opposite churchmen who consider it inexpedient in this modern time to take a hard line are sentimentally occupying the same pews sat in so many years ago by those judges who saw no harm in making bishops not apostles but moral clerks. They provide the alternative to the "mere Christians" and their Church as a ponderous social institution alongside the school or hospital is poles apart from the apocalyptic Jerusalem which is the flesh and spirit of the Church married to Christ, the bride which made St. Augustine say, "When I talk about her I cannot stop."[1]

* * *

The Church began to measure its steps in 1944 when the Bishop of Hong Kong and South China, R. O. Hall, ordained a woman to the priesthood. The Archbishops of Canterbury and York at once repudiated the ordination and the woman's priestly ministry was annulled. In 1948 the business was revived at the Eighth Lambeth Conference which received a proposal originating in the same Diocese of Hong Kong and South China.

That proposal recommended a plan by which "for an experimental period of twenty years a deaconess might (subject to certain conditions) be ordained to the priesthood." The Lambeth bishops rejected it with the statement that "the Conference feels bound to reply that in its opinion such an experiment would be against the tradition and order (within the Anglican Communion) and would gravely affect the internal and external relations of the Anglican Communion."

On the other hand, recognizing apparent Scriptural approval of deaconesses, however ambiguous that term may have been used, and realizing that the diaconate was a fully separate order with no particular consequence for interpretations of sacerdotal and Eucharistic theology, the same Conference reaffirmed "Resolution 67 of the Conference of 1930 that 'the Order of Deaconesses is for women the one and only Order of the Ministry which we can recommend our branch of the Catholic Church to recognize and use.'"

Thus Lambeth reaffirmed its Catholic claims and recognized the weight of those claims upon ordinal reforms. In a slightly anticlimactic action, three advisors (Michael Ramsey, J.J. Carpenter and C.F.D. Moule) presented to a twelve-man committee formed by the Convocations of Canterbury and York in 1953 the opinion that Scriptures do not prevent women from leading the Daily Offices. The ease of this decision and the position on deaconesses at Lambeth VIII indicated that theological difficulty in the ordination of women was present only in relation to the particular office of priest; the problem was with the sacerdotal, and not pastoral, ministry.

The real confrontation between classical ideas of the Scriptures, Church and Eucharist came to the fore at Lambeth X in 1968. The Dean of York, Alan Richardson, wrote in a preparatory paper for the Committee on Women and the Priesthood that the most important of the theological arguments concerning the ordination of women concerns the nature of the priesthood itself. In the body of his presentation, the Dean introduced the conciliar argument by questioning

> Whether such a decision taken by a single separate branch of the Church (for example, the Anglican Communion) could possess such authority; it would not be reverting to an ancient practice (as, for example, restoring the Cup to the laity) but would be making an innovation for which there was no ancient or ecumenical precedent. This is the critical question which underlies the debate whether the Anglican Communion should proceed to the ordination of women to the priesthood now. It is a profoundly theological question, since it raises the issue of authority in the separated branches of the universal Church of Christ. The fundamental ... question concerns the theological propriety of an innovation within one branch of the historic Church, lacking the consensus of the whole Church.[2]

Considering the clergy shortage in most parts of the Anglican Communion, a shortage almost burlesqued by the opposite deployment problem in much of the United States, he added that manpower shortage as a justification for the ordination of priestesses would be the worst of all possible reasons for the innovation. Here was the heart of the problem: theological truth cannot be determined by social expediency. Consequently, even if we style the priesthood as professional, its norms must not be determined by the norms of professionalism.

The Dean of York and his archbishop were dramatically at odds. Then again, that has long been a matter of gentlemanly form with bishops and deans. The Archbishop, Donald Coggan, usually a supreme biblicist, defended his support of women in the priesthood by saying that the Conference was not to be insulted "with silly arguments about our Lord having no women in the Apostolic Twelve." Of course, if what Our Lord made of the Twelve is "silly" may not the fact of the "Twelve" at all be silly? Apparently, those who are heirs of the spiritualia of the Twelve, bishops — and archbishops — draw the line there.

At any rate, that was a passing remark and the Archbishop continued although his manner of presentation came under strong criticism from Trevor Huddleston, among others. Inasmuch as the Church of Scotland virtually owes its existence to the rejection of the Catholic claims of the Church of England, the Archbishop then descended to the greatest depths of irrelevance by citing the action of the Scottish Presbyterians a few months earlier in opening its ministry to women. Contrary to Oliver Cromwell's feeling that "presbyter is priest writ large," they are not the same and neither Presbyterians nor Anglicans pretend as much. Unless one is a latitudinarian sort, one must recognize that the ordinal canons of Protestantism have no relevance to the Anglican case or to Catholicism in general.

Recognition of this at the Conference came from two priests not ordinarily considered a sympathetic pair. They were Metropolitan Parthenios, Orthodox patriarch of Alexandria and Metropolitan of Carthage, who did not consider the matter worthy of debate, and Marcus Loane, Archbishop of Sydney. Said Sydney in a pointed reference to York: "It *is* significant that there is no New Testament precedent for the ordination of women." He went on to say that "there is a distinction in the function which the Persons of the Godhead fulfill," and repeated the position that equality and subordination exist in the Trinity side by side. "There is a distinction in function as there is in human life. To do what the Report proposes (i.e., the proposal of Dr. Coggan's committee to ordain women to the priesthood) would be in conflict with the doctrine of the Godhead. As God has made men and God has made women, there is a function for each — and I believe in order."

Later, in a supreme manifestation of the "mere Christian" confounding the old party lables, it was this traditionally styled "Evangelical" who rejected the free advice of the Congregational representative that the Anglican Communion should fully open its highest ministries to women. In an attitude of complete modesty which turned out to be completely necessary, that representative argued that since the Congregational bodies in England had been ordaining women to the ministry with success for the past fifty years, the Anglicans had an encouraging precedent. The Archbishop simply observed: "What is right in the Congregational Church has no bearing on the matter. The doctrine of the ministry in the Catholic Church is totally different... Those who want to have women priests are acting from sentiment... My view is based on Scriptures and what we hold as the historic ministry." With these words from Sydney, some may have imagined, somewhere above London, Bucer and St. Vincent shaking hands.

* * *

Five resolutions of the Tenth Lambeth Conference (Nos. 34-38) dealt with women in the priesthood. The Archbishop of York's position was defeated. His original wording for Resolution 34: "There are, in principle, no conclusive theological reasons for withholding priesthood from women." The revision approved by the bishops read: "The Conference affirms its opinion that the theological arguments as at present presented for and against the ordination of women to the priesthood are inconclusive." The next three resolutions made the Anglican Consultative Council an agency for further discussion. The final resolution recognized the tradition of deaconesses by recommending that the several Churches provide "for duly qualified women to share in the conduct of liturgical worship, to preach, to baptize, to read the Epistle and Gospel at the Holy Communion and to help in the distribution of the elements."

The Anglican Consultative Council took its assignment seriously. Meeting in 1971 in Kenya the Council dealt with the ordination of women in three resolutions. First, it called for all Anglican Churches to report their view for "consideration" by the Anglican Consultative Council in 1973; second, it narrowly voted to give Synods the initiative in the matter so that a bishop with the consent of his synod, would have the sympathy of the Council should he ordain a priestess; Third, it asked Metropolitans and Primates to consult other Churches for opinions.

The Council was occupied with the possibility that the Bishop of Hong Kong, Gilbert Baker, continuing the tradition of his see, would attempt the ordination of a woman. This factor gave its actions added portent. The idea of synodical initiative, passed by the Council in direct opposition to the theory of ecumenical conciliarism we have discussed, was rejected by the 1971 Council of the Church of South-East Asia which, in response to a request from the Bishop of Hong Kong for a ruling on the issue of women, passed a nearly unanimous resolution to refrain from action until all the provinces of the Anglican Communion have submitted reports, presumably in 1973. The Council of the Church in South-East Asia includes the Dioceses in Malaysia, Singapore, the Philippines, Hong Kong, Taiwan, Korea and Burma along with the Philippine Independent Church. The clerical delegates, sitting separately, had earlier decided by a unanimous vote not to ordain women to the priesthood. Nevertheless, repeating the action of his predecessor in 1944, the Bishop of Hong Kong in November, 1971 ordained two women to the style of priest.

* * *

The question is only in abeyance. Before the Hong Kong ordination, the interdenominational English Society for the Ministry of Women in the Church had stated that "the Society looks forward to the probability of Deaconess Jane Hwang, of Hong Kong, becoming before long the first woman to be ordained priest in the Anglican Communion." The report continues to say that in the light of the Methodist decision on reunion with the Church of England and the possible breach in Anglican resistance, "this year has certainly marked significant steps forward. It now seems possible that the goal for which we have been working so long is likely to be reached within the foreseeable future within the main Churches outside the Roman and Orthodox Communions."[3]

Those last few words are the stranglehold. Bearing in mind the facts so muted in the above statement that "the main Churches outside the Roman Catholic and Orthodox Communions" are but a minority of Christendom and, on the whole, never have made the sacerdotal claims which make the ordination of women in the Anglican Communion a stumbling block, we must ask if ordination of women is truly ecumenical or Catholic at all. This thought at least tempered the 1970 General Convention of the American Episcopal Church which voted for ordination of women to the diaconate but not to the priesthood. The Dutch Old Catholic representative at Lambeth X, Van Kleef, indicated that his church would consider Anglican approval of priestesses "with great regret and embarrassment." The situation would be grievously more strained with the Latin and Orthodox Churches. This is not a bureaucratic matter, but one of the most indicting theological matters ever to confront Anglicanism. Our actions will decide for the rest of Christendom whether our claim to be Reformed and Catholic has been valid or whether it has been a dexterous posture enabling us to be Protestants in copes.

Chapter VII

THE BIBLE

"It's a poor sort of memory that only works backwards," sniffed the Queen in *Through the Looking-Glass*. If the Church is to be the Church, however, it must confound the Queen and all others for whom the facts of the past are an embarrassment. Certainly that must be the course for Anglicanism in consideration of its practice of Scriptural testimony:

> The Church hath power to decree Rites or Ceremonies, and authority in Controversies of Faith: And yet it is not lawful for the Church to ordain anything that is contrary to God's Word written, neither may it so expound one place of Scripture, that it is repugnant to another. Wherefore, although the Church be a witness and a keeper of holy Writ, yet, as it ought not to decree any thing against the same, so besides the same ought it not to enforce any thing to be believed for necessity of Salvation."[1]

As pointed out earlier, the Vicentian Canon is abrogated whenever Scriptural tradition is ignored. So Anglicans have spoken to Rome in reference to papal claims. Gregory Baum recently defended those claims by classifying them "not biblical doctrine" as such but the Spirit-centered, Scripture-tested experience of the Church, out of which she verbalizes what is the modern meaning of the Gospel. Hans Kung directly challenged this position, asserting that it is an outright return to the Roman Catholic "developmental" thinking which was "essentially a questionable product of nineteenth century Tubingen theology.[2]

If we are to be faithful to Catholic practice there is no doubt that the Church must be the channel of Spirited change and generation; that is the light which inspires the coupling of Scripture and tradition, of faith and practice. But she is a disingenuous channel if she does not remain faithful to Scriptural revelation. We are back to Vincent of Lerins: the theologian's task is to speak *non nova sed nove,* not of new things but of old things newly.

For Kung, as well as for Anglicanism, the vagaries of Fr. Baum's phrase compromise the proper acceptance of Scriptures as the decisive *norma normans non normata.* Cumulative tradition or, more seriously, private fancy, is valueless without the agreement of Scripture. We cannot afford the independent luxury of the Oxford don who began a sermon, "As St. Paul once said, and I am inclined to agree with him . . . "

* * *

If one asks what the Biblical norm is for the ordination of priestesses, one may get three answers. Inasmuch as the New Testament does not speak of Christian priestesses, it is ambiguous and therefore not opposed, or blinded by cultural prejudice and therefore to be ignored, or clearly and willfully opposed and therefore to be heeded.

First, arguments of ambiguity which open the way to consent by omission are dangerous. Christians have enslaved each other from age to age from Carthage to Rhode Island because the New Testament did not expressly forbid institutional slavery, either.

Second, and more important, is the question of cultural bias. Unless one is willing to admit the possibliity that the exclusion of women had as much theological purposiveness as the inclusion of the Gentiles, one must take the difficult position that the Church which "liberated" the Gentiles at great pain to its Jewishness succumbed to chauvinism in the face of women. Of course, there is the possibility that it never occurred to the Christian women to petition. Yielding, however, to the discipline of a memory cursed to work backwards, we see that this does not stand up. According to Acts 21, St. Paul, of all people, lived for some days in the same house with four female preachers. A third of all the church people listed with especial affection in the last chapter of Romans is women. In Romans, Paul calls Phoebe a specially titled "deaconess" of the church at Cenchrea, although we must carefully remark that the Greek word *diakonos* is a very general one and its use in Romans does not necessarily imply a formal order; it seems in any case to have set precedent because deaconesses as a special order continued to exist until about the eleventh century. Regardless, Phoebe here holds some office of special trust, possibly the defense of Paul before the secular authorities. Clearly, women were not shy; certainly not women bold enough to be Christians in the first place and certainly not the mothers of all the Monicas and Helenas of history.

Is it possible that the one peculiar office of priestess did not occur to them? Extravagant as it may seem, that might be admissable were we not once again burdened by a memory that works backwards. Quite simply, the idea of women in a priesthood was infinitely more apparent to those living in the world of early Christianity than it is to us. In a world whose mountains homed gods and goddesses, incense was offered by priestesses as well as priests before Delphi, Cybele and Artemis. There is nothing new about that at all. It had even become part of Semitic tradition.

Not only before but also after the Hebrew conquest in the second millenium B.C., a Mother Goddess, presumably attended by priestesses and priests, was worshipped in Palestine; so say the Ras Shamra tablets in their record of a Syrian version of the Mesopotamian Tammuz-Ishtar myth which was called the Baal-Anat Epic. Since anthropologists and commentators allow that Mt. Carmel originally was a sanctuary of the Canaanite deity Aleyan-Baal and the home of that sort of cultus, it is thoroughly probable that the "prophets of the groves four hundred, which eat at Jezebel's table" were priestesses of the goddess Asherah. Elijah's fire most likely prevailed against priestesses as well as priests.3

Ezekiel spoke of women weeping in the Temple for Tammuz, and Jeremiah along with Hosea and Amos all attacked cults nurtured by priestesses. The Mosaic attention to covenant by circumcision may have effectively rendered women insufficient attendants in the worship of the right God of the Temple yet Christianity changed even that. Water baptism eliminated sexual requirements for initiation. This is the holy truth in St. Paul that there is no male or female. Still, this Christianity of Hellenized Jews avoided the tradition of priestesses firmly established in their Graeco-Roman world and remembered in the lore of the Jewish histories. In the presence of the Greek philosophies,

> ... the decisive question was whether Jesus Christ would turn out to be the decisive fact for understanding the human situation in the world, or whether the current world-understandings would, in the end, place the things concerning Jesus Christ in *their* context. That is to say, would the current mythology determine the understanding of the things concerning Jesus Christ, or would the things concerning Jesus Christ be able to assert their fact-like properties sufficiently to make a decisive and definitive modification of the mythology.4

Love places because of things, not things because of places advised Gregory the Great five hundred years afterward; Paul said as much as he Christianized the best of the Gentile world. Tertullian may have asked what Athens had to do with Jerusalem; Paul did not. The avoidance of priestesses in Gentile Christianity was precisely that: avoidance and not mere omission. In the face of the openness of the Church in the process of Hellinization, such avoidance is not only significant, it is dramatic. We cannot ignore the simple observation of Archbishop Athenagoras: "Our poor Lord did not include in His cabinet of twelve any of those women who contributed with their substance for His sustinence." We can only add that neither did His Greek followers.

* * *

Anyone turning to Scripture for evidence and certainly anyone subscribing to a Catholic understanding of Holy Orders, must at once recognize that the subject of the ordination of women is far too comprehensive to be dealt with as a simple matter of general ministry. Given the order of ranks in the ministry and the fundamental understanding of the peculiar sacramental responsibilities of the priesthood, there is a great difference between ordination to the diaconate and ordination to the priesthood or episcopate; the former is essentially pastoral in responsibility while the latter two are outrightly sacramental. *Presbyteros* (priest) and *episkopos* (bishop) are used practically interchangeably in the New Testament; they are never confused with *diakonos*.[5]

The Dutch Catechism is gravely in error if, by calling the diaconate a grade of the priesthood, it means that it is not a degree of the general priesthood of all believers but an organic part of the specific sacerdotal offices.[6] This is much the same confusion that we find in Dr. Macquarrie's *Principles of Christian Theology* and explains why his opposition to the ordination of priestesses is based on conciliar authority and not Scriptural witness. Considering the diaconate organically related to the higher offices, he concludes, "... while it is true that the fact of there having been 'deaconesses' in both the earlier and more recent periods of Church history makes it easier to visualize the admission of women to the diaconate, this order is continuous with those above it, and in principle there would be no barrier to advancement on the grounds of sex alone."[7]

What sacramental rights appertain to the diaconate (e.g., assisting at the Eucharist and, in a certain sense, preaching) are the property of the general priesthood of all believers and are not at all "continuous" with the particular duties of the priest and bishop. Therefore it would be entirely possible and consistent to ordain deaconesses while preventing the ordination of priestesses. These orders are organically separate, fully unlike the difference between a vice-president and a president and absolutely unfamiliar to the ordained Protestant ministries whose divisions are defined according to pastoral and administrative, rather than sacramental, responsibility.

It is sometimes difficult, because of misleading modern practice, to remember that the apostolic episcopate is supremely sacerdotal, the bishop being the chief sacramental officer of the diocese; the episcopate is not fundamentally an administrative office. It is an historical fact that the only order which has administration as its definitive attention is the diaconate; in the formative years of the Church's order, the deacons were the administrative functionaries of the bishop's household, assisting him in his sacerdotal work by assuming the burden of practical business supervision. Their work required more than the eucharistic offices of the priests who were essentially the sacramental vicars of the bishop. Thus it was that deacons, although fewer in number than priests, were "full-time" clergy much more commonly in the first two centuries of the Church than were priests, who were, for the most part, what we should today call "non-stipendiary." The situation has a ring familiar to many modern situations.

* * *

Besides Cornelius, who was Bishop of Rome from 251 to 253, there were among the church officers of his city forty-six presbyters, seven deacons, seven sub-deacons, forty-two acolytes and fifty-two exorcists, readers and door-keepers; a numerical classification of minor orders was established in the Middle Ages but varied even then in some places. St. Thomas Aquinas, later reaffirmed by the Council of Trent, justified the singular status of the priest in this vast delegation on the grounds of his peculiar right to consecrate the Sacrament. This is the constant identity of the priest and obviously explains why his office has never been subject to the vicissitudes of the others. His order was as fundamental to the life of the Church as the life-giving Eucharist, unlike the diaconate which in the early Church was altered by administrative requirements. A.J.B.

Higgins, in a commentary on 1 Timothy, discounts the presence of deaconesses at the time of that letter altogether and believes that the only real counterparts of deacons were widows. Manson, on the other hand, writing on Romans, clearly believes that the formal diaconate could be, and was, shared by men and women in the early apostolic church.[8] The disagreement between these two is simple evidence of the unsettled and evolutionary nature of this order. The presence of the priesthood is another matter:

> In striking contrast with the diaconate, the presbyterate can hardly be said to be introduced at all ... If to institute an order of deacons marked a step in development, it is evident that, to the mind of the historian of Acts, the appointment of presbyters did not mark anything at all. It seems to have been too much a matter of course to be even worth mentioning.[9]

Arguments for excluding priestesses may likewise have seemed too obvious to the early Church to have been mentioned. Not until the fourth century, for instance, do we find any written grounds justifying the exclusion of the Virgin from the priesthood.[10] Such omission can be portentous. Certainly, if the New Testament cannot be said to consent by silence to priestesses, and if it is not the prejudiced commentary of a particularly stifling culturism, we must conclude that its case is manifestly theological.

This outline of the priest-deacon relationship can alter custom in an unexpected way. Assuming that theological arguments against the ordination of priestesses do not apply to deaconesses since they are a fully different entity, it is entirely possible that the local churches of the twentieth century could be fully "administered" by women assuming, as deaconesses, most of the governing responsibilities now charged by the bishop to priests. Most rectors complain that so much of their time is spent on matters for which one does not need to be a priest. It would be possible to have a parish "rectored" by a woman in deaconess' orders, assisted by priests, stipendiary or no. Priests would be free to be priests. The problem is that we are so clerical, so prelatical and essentially so apart from a right Catholic mind, that we continue to confuse sacerdotalism with clericalism, making priest synonymous with rector. Our opposition should be to the priestess, not to the rectoress.

If there is any part of the whole ordinal question in which we may be governed by sheer utilitarian concerns it is the diaconate because pragmatic service is its very function. Consider the miraculous activity of Dorothy Kerin, Anglican stigmatist and healer who, until her death in 1962, presided over her own foundation of a healing center in England.[11] The highest administrative office sanctioned by the Anglican Church at the present time happens to be held by a woman, the Queen of England. Shortly before receiving the Sword of State at her coronation, the Monarch put on the Supertunica, resembling the diaconal dalmatic, just as Carthusian nuns traditionally receive diaconal stoles and maniples at their profession. She then heard the Archbishop's charge, reminiscent of the bishop's examination of deacons in the Prayer Book, to "protect the Holy Church of God, help and defend widows and orphans, restore the things that are gone to decay, maintain the things that are restored, punish and reform what is amiss, and confirm what is in good order." This is something women have often done far better, and it is something for which a priest is not needed. So the Mother Church of Anglicanism symbolically maintains, in full Catholicity, a woman as its administrative head, the defender of Church as well as of State. Women in rectorships have been part of Anglican practice from the Elizabethan Compromise to the present.

Chapter VIII

NEITHER UP NOR DOWN

There has never been a time when Christians did not call God, Father. Jesus taught us that and He himself spoke of Abba, or Papa, an intimacy which should make us afraid of His mind and what it knew.

Father is a title proper not for just the first person of the Trinity in deference to the facts of his innascibility and spiration; it may also be used for the Holy Trinity collectively in acknowledgement of the initiatory and generative function of the Trinity within the universe. This masculinity is the property of the Son and Holy Spirit as well as of the Father who, as *Auto-theos,* supports their existence. Thus, for example, the Holy Spirit is as much "He" as the Father or the Son, in spite of the fact that the apocryphal Acts of Thomas called the Holy Spirit in one of its hymns "Divine Mother" since the Aramaic word for spirit, "rouah," is feminine.

That the Father supports the existence of Son and Holy Spirit in no way denigrates them. This is true in the same sense that the Filoque clause of the Nicene creed establishes no inequality between the Son and the Holy Spirit. Consequently, reference that the Holy Spirit proceeds from the Son, a doctrine affirmed in the Nicene Creed amended in 589 by the Council of Toledo, is absent from the credal texts of the Eastern churches and modern Western translations with no injury to the equal dignity of the two, although the Eastern Orthodox legitimately question what wrong things it might unwittingly suggest about the relationship between Father and Son.

This maleness is not an expression of mere convenience; it is part of the essence of Christianity. No canonical Christian writing has ever called God "She" or "It." That must be a weighty factor in the discussion and not an observation of mere custom. Inevitably, elimination of sexual reference to the Godhead has indicated the presence of a non-Christian bias for, worse than making God impersonal, it depersonalizes Him. The great confrontation of existential Christian theology with the pure Aristotelian philosophy of a Prime-Mover quite mechanical and non-personal, resulted in some attempts at apologizing the Christian revelation to the Greek mind by neuterizing God. We know, for example, that Aristedes of Athens informed Hadrian (117-38) in his *Apology* that the Christian God had no sex.[1] In Arius's *Confession* presented to his Bishop in 321 AD. the use of "Father" is deliberately avoided. Even Gregory of Nazianzus was inclined to treat masculine language about God as an awkward metaphor. Obviously, the paternity of God dismayed sophisticated ancients as it does many today; there is perhaps no greater proof that the Trinity is not a Greek philosophical fancy than the blatant sexuality of the Trinitarian formula.

Religion cerebralized will always show itself in objections to divine sex because the very concept, expressing as it does the intimate relevance of God to man, affronts the idea that God, if He exists at all, is a passive observer whose chief function is to set things in motion and provide some sense of order. Revelation becomes morality, righteousness becomes deportments and it all becomes as sensible as the Jefferson Bible — and no more authentic to Gospel witness.

The First Directory during the French Revolution saw such fanciful attempts at neo-classical rationalism as Felix le Pelletier's "Patheonistes," Daubermesnil's "culte des adorateurs" and Benoist-Lamothe's social cult with its bread of fraternity and patronage of the "sage of Galilee." Priestesses had full status with priests, a woman representing Reason was enthroned on the altar of Notre Dame and a new calendar was introduced, replacing the Sabbath week with a more symmetrical decade. Thus was confirmed the spirit by means of which, wrote one historian, "extreme Republicans hoped to gratify at once their hatred of Christianity and their passion for the decimal system."[3] The united deist movement called "Theanthropisme" made official the break with Christian "anthropomorphism" and God was given a rest home in the sky. In Robespierre's 1794 oration on "The Festival of the Supreme Being," although paternity is given lip-service, only the exigencies of French grammar prevented "the Being" from being called "It."

The most basic truths are expressed in the most basic ways. The life-giving of Christ comes to us in bread and wine and water. When we worship God who is real in creation we use our bodies; honest worship is a sexual action. The whitewashed austerity of churches designed as lecture halls cannot last. When men worship a God who is real they must light fires and dance, and this they have done from long before David's dance right up to all the solemn pacings at High Mass à la Fortescue. We have regularly tried our hand at overcoming this nature; Michal called David vulgar and the Victorian Ritual Commission had a few "advanced" vicars arrested. As long as men are men, though, David's defense is sufficient: "I will make merry before the Lord."[4]

The coincidence cannot escape our attention: those systems in which sexuality has not been important have invariably rejected the understanding of a God immanent in the affairs of men. One Quaker psychoanalyst has observed: "Real knowledge, real understanding of the world must *ultimately* be sexual. Freud and the orthodox analysts adopted this viewpoint rigidly. They insisted that all attempts to understand man and his conflicts in other terms, such as Jung's religious archetypes, Adler's drive for power, or Rank's birth trauma, were necessarily superficial and misleading. At its most fundamental level life must be interpreted in sexual terms . . . "[5] If John Smith calls his father Mr. Smith you may well question the closeness of their relationship. So it is with Christianity which claims a bold intimacy between man and God. The great masters of prayer have rarely availed themselves of such literary flowers as "the Almighty" or "the Supreme Being"; invariably in the natural breath of prayer they said with Christ the same name He may have called as a child across Joseph's workbench: Abba.

The Christian must ask if our sense of the gender God, the sense which lets us say Abba, is anything less than vitally true in the corpus of fundamental Christian belief. English schoolboys sing this song:

> The noble Duke of York,
> He had ten thousand men,
> He marched them up to the top of the hill
> And he marched them down again.
> And when they were up they were up,
> And when they were down they were down,
> And when they were only half way up
> They were neither up nor down.

If God is to be more than the eternal "It" of the Deist, Unitarian and Stoic mind, if He is to be the lofty Creator whose presence is both in the heavens and in the prints of the Redeemer on earth. He must be sensate. A God who claims no sexual language is not the God of experience revelation: He is neither "up nor down." He divests himself of the divine majesty and becomes, as P.M. Dawley used to say, a figure like Strephon in "Iolanthe" who manages to be half fairy and half man; the fairy part of Strephon could fly through keyholes but his legs got stuck. So it was with the Christ of the Nestorians, that learned group of early heretics who rationalized that Jesus must have been half human and half divine, in other words, neither up nor down. That was the cry of the prominent New York priest who during a sermon orated before a crucifix: "There He hangs before you, half man and half God." It unites those who say Christ never ascended into the heavens with those who say He never went to the toilet. It makes perfect sense but it is not the Gospel.

To dispense with the maleness of God is also to dispense with some of the most profound mystical language of the scriptures. The failure of Christian preachers to deal intelligently with such language may have been part of the price paid for the disassociation of Christian revelation from the concerns of church polity in the last few generations. It is also a mark of our sexual wilderness out of which a new generation is trying to wander, albeit not often in a Christian light but certainly with an affirmation of the scriptural identity of body and soul, flesh and spirit, as a mysterious unity. Every time we are moved by music, poetry or architecture we evidence this truth; Christian healing could not take place were it not so. In fact, the entire sacramental system without this unity is complete wash. "The Church," wrote Donald Baillie, "must indeed break out continually into ... lyrical notes to make up for the shortcomings of theological prose, and no expression can be too high. Nothing can be too high; and nothing can be too lowly or too human. Nothing can be too high, if only we save it from Docetic and Monophysite unreality by treating His life as in every sense a human life. A toned down Christology is absurd. It must be all or nothing — all or nothing on both the divine and the human side."[6]

This Christ-mysticism is the most terrific concreteness, as hard as nails and as real as living and dying. Only the Christian can know, with every pound of the hammer and every surprised Easter shout, the full ache and shine of reality: "We have seen the Lord." Superstition and escape are the games of the world: "Tell people, 'His disciples came by night and stole Him away while we were asleep.'"[7]

God may have been hailed as the "Supreme Being" in the neo-classical glades of the French revolutionary cults and He is frequently so addressed today in the pieties of Presidential prayer breakfasts and oratorical competitions. He is never so named in the Bible. He has more feeling than that: He is what He is, Yahweh, but what He is is Creator; He cannot be without creating because He is life itself. He is father and lover and king, rebuker and reconciler. He is not the founder of the Church, He is the Bridegroom of the Church. The central act of the Church on earth, the Eucharist, is not a celebration of life and genius that was the sport of the Greek Cynics and the French

Decadistes. It is a more festal and more awesome thing: it is a marriage supper, The Wedding Feast. This is the supernatural action in which God who conferred his sensuality upon creation by breathing on primordial water fleshes our senses with lights and incense and color and, above all, bread and wine, marrying invisibility with visibility and ritually consummating the marriage proposed in Adam, contracted in Abraham and sealed in Christ. This is the Christian romance: that divinity and humanity should have courted in a garden, spoken plain sense together out in the open and then published the consummation in the three languages of Empire: Jesus of Nazareth, King of the Jews. Jesus Man and Christ God, all together, with one foot in Genesis and one in Revelation, at home in that green garden and in the gold city. "This is a great mystery," said St. Paul, "but I speak of Christ and His Church."[8]

* * *

God has given us bodies and a language to match them. We speak of men and women for that is what we are. If God created both men and women in His own image, then it is certain that His sexuality is comprehensive; that is to say, the fundamental principle of life requires both what our language calls male and female attributes. What Henri Bergson said in the *Creative Evolution* is infinitely truer of God than of us: "There is no manifestation of life which does not contain in a rudimentary state — either latent or potential — the essential characteristcs of most other manifestations."[9] Superficially, this would indicate confusion and that is certainly the human risk. Noel Coward once told Dorothy Parker, dressed in heavy tweeds, that she almost looked like a man; "so do you," she replied. God can manage much more satisfactorily. In Him is both cosmic act and response, masculine initiation and feminine fulfillment, for He is perfect love and hence both initiatory and sustaining. It is a great mistake, however, to confuse this co-mingling with reduction or neuterization. Nor is it mere

"role-playing" as Milton pictured it:
> For spirits when they please
> Can either sex assume, or both; so soft
> And uncompounded is their essence pure.[10]

This naivete was repeated recently at a meeting of feminists in New York at which a copy of Michelangelo's Sistine Chapel painting of God touching the finger of Adam was shown with God repainted as a goddess of Rubinesque proportions.

The co-mingling of sexual attributes in God in heaven is as great a mystery as the specific sex of God in His dealing with men, in the relationship between Christ and His Church. The difference is that the former vision is beyond our ken and evidently is apocalyptic, outside the chronology of our experience and properly revealed, if at all, in the Final Revelation itself when God no longer interacts with time. "Now we see through a glass darkly, but then face to face."[11] The nature of God is, in an allegorical way, like the perfection of Beatrice in the Divine Comedy. Dante wrote in the third tractate of the *Convivio:* "We cannot look fixedly upon her aspect because the soul is so intoxicated by it that after gazing it at once goes astray."[12] This is no neuter creation at all but is so powerfully beyond our present capacity to understand, so beyond our normal thought patterns which are necessarily conditioned by the temporal conditions of cause and effect, action and reaction, that, while being sensible, it leaves us senseless. So St. Simeon wrote: "When we attain perfection, God ... comes under a certain image, and yet it is the image of God. For God does not appear in any figure or sign whatever, but makes himself seen in his simplicity, formed out of formless, incomprehensible light. I can say no more."

Just as the perfection of Beatrice must be clothed in mortality to be comprehensible, so must all our Christian language be clothed if it is to make human sense. That is so not because the God with whom we deal is sexless; we could easily comprehend that. It is so because God is sexual to a degree utterly incomprehensible to us. He is what He is. He is both seminal initiator and maternal cultivator of life without being hermaphroditic and He is lustless without being a eunuch. He created man and woman both in His image and yet has always come to us as a man.

> The mystics tell us that nothing we can say about God can be other than misleading, and perhaps we are chattering too much about him. "God is in heaven and thou upon earth, therefore let thy words be few." Yet out of the darkness of mystery the light shines, out of the infinite silence the word is spoken. Because of the Christ-event and its consequences, Christians know God and worship him in unashamedly personal categories as the God and Father of Jesus Christ . . . The loving Father of Christian faith and experience is still the mysterious and transcendent Other beyond all our conceiving and imagining in the mystery of his eternal being. Christians know God "in the face of Christ," and this is the test of all revelation through whatever channels it may be thought to come.[13]

Whatever the incomprehensible mystery behind all this is, it has been the divine wisdom to make His personality comprehensible to us in the language of mortality which calls Him a man, and a Father. The ominous thing for those who would underestimate this language is that it is not a language of mere convenience; it is the language of experience. He did not just let us call Him He, He showed Himself as He and taught us to call Him our Father. We see God the way we do because of that. It is no simple subjectivism. Speaking of the prophet Hosea's imagery for God, C.H. Dodd in one place acknowledges that Hosea, being a man, is making God in his own image but he then asks who made Hosea such a man. Hosea's own reply is that "the same mysterious act of grace made him such as he was and made him see that God is such as He is."[14]

That is all we know of our personal intercourse with God but it must be our textbook more than gynecology or psychology. It is the one thing we have to go on. Gerardus Van der Leeuw, who wrote so beautifully about sublimity saw this as a simple truth: "We must not judge the Bible by Greek anthropology or modern epistemology; on the contrary, we must develop our anthropology and epistemology from what revelation teaches us about ourselves."15

Chapter IX

THE ICON OF CHRIST

The institution of the priesthood is, like the institution of the Church, a type of the great paradox or *skandalon* of Christianity: both represent a meeting of the noumenal and the phenomenal, the entrance of the eschaton into history. What most readily affronts us about such things is not the presence of the divine, but the presence of the human. What is supernatural offends our romantic desires by seeming no more than crudely superhuman, in the manner of the early Greek gods. We feel vulgarized as did Plato.

For example, the continuing debate about the "spiritual Church" and the "institutional Church" has come to a sharp focus in our own day. It has long been the cry of both the petty anti-clericalist and the legitimate reformer. Fundamentally, it is always a dualist conceit. The assumption that a Church "institutionalized" must be of a lower order than a Church "underground" or "without walls" courts the dangerous sentiment that formalism must always be Pharasaic and that earthly forms cannot adequately be "Spiritual." Referring to a dictum of Ignatius of Antioch, the French liturgical scholar Louis Bouyer has said quite plainly that an invisible Church is the same thing as no Church at all.[1]

If we remember that ours is the proclamation of the God-Man, we can avoid mistaking supernatural sacramentalism for superhuman activity. If we believe with Bruce Barton or those who preach "the power of positive thinking" that Christ's great strength was His talent with men and that His smile, if seen today, could seal the most awkward corporation contract and that His handshake would do a Rotarian proud, then we would be superhumanists and legitimately open to attack. We would be remiss as Christians if this did not offend us ourselves. It certainly has every reason to cause offense. As but one example, you will notice how those who most strongly believe in the superhuman are the most patronizing in aspect. In their conversations to attempt friendship they usually give no indication that anyone has a last name, and they slap you on the back as if they were General Lee slapping the haunches of his faithful "Traveller." Simple things, but they indicate a dilemma. When we are superhumanists, humility will always be a patronism because, for the superhuman, it can only possible exist as an affectation. That is why the evidence of humility takes on such extravagant display in the churches: bishops, for instance, with homespun vestments and carrying croziers carved by some fully authenticated shepherd outfitter. There is no idea of a distinction between office and man; the person who minimizes the ritual embellishments of his office and ultimately the institution itself is asserting the most self-conscious individualism, full in the belief that all the veneration is for him and him alone and therefore, for the sake of appearance, to be eliminated. Every so often the stage gives birth to an actor who thinks he actually is Hamlet. That makes for a counterfeit Hamlet and, quite worse, no actor at all.

We shall not approach the priesthood in the right way unless we realize that it is not superhuman but supernatural. Because of that, its supernatural integrity depends on the thorough humanity of its priests without regard for their talents and is not dissolved by a lack of personal credit, just as the Incarnation required the humanity of God but could have been effected just as readily had Christ been a deaf mute. It would not be the best situation but it would still be real. In the priesthood is re-enacted the befuddling interplay and fellowship of the divine and the earthly. As a result, it is bound to be an impractical office; many Christian sects have tried to manage without it and many Catholic Christians have regretted it. But Christianity being what it is, something may be impractical and still necessary. As a profession it may be an enigma and its historical development may appear ambiguous. It will not impress the superhumanist. Yet, as Yves Congar has said, the main argument for it is not so much historical as theological.[2] We have it, not because we are superhumanly good at it, but because God made it necessary.

Cuthbert Simpson, of the General Theological Seminary and later Dean of Christ Church, Oxford, was known throughout the Church, either by report or by unforgettable experience, as a man whose bluntness could both chasten and profoundly embarrass a situation. He was a rare image of the sort of greatness more usually identified with the age of Wilberforce or the like rather than our own age of collectivism. That means he was not easily categorized by that new stereotyping facility called "image." It has been recorded how this man who could terrify pompous souls could also come to tears in the course of an ordination sermon as he preached the inadequacy of young men in the face of their Orders.

That is the sort of thing we mean by holy awe. It does not make a man Samson tearing down the pillars; it makes him Jesus building a new kingdom with a few fishermen, a tax collector and the like. "Vows can't change nature," said Robert Browning. "Priests are only men."[3] That is the whole point. Humanity is not an inadvertent obstacle to the priesthood nor does it have to be "overcome." Its weakness, like the weakness of the Church, is a proclamation of the irony of the Incarnation, that the Son of God who promises a heavenly Jerusalem should have to weep over a city only 2500 feet wide and that the builder of Jerusalem should be one carpenter. So for fishers of men, Christ chooses just fishermen.

Talk of "improving" the priesthood by removing its sexual requirements is a Docetism as romantically superhuman as that which engages plans for a non-institutional Church, free of the trivia of administration. It places the burden of integrity on the individual's talents rather than on the simple fact of his sexual existence, scorning the Messianic precedent which chose a specifically masculine human nature with all its limitations for the earthly representative of the High Priesthood of Christ

Himself.

Now inasmuch as all Christians are initiated into the Body of Christ it is certainly true that both men and women manifest divinity in our humanity and thus together stand before the Father as priests freely returning to Him creation. "Here we offer and present unto thee, O Lord, ourselves, our souls and bodies, to be a reasonable, holy and living sacrifice unto thee."[4] St. Augustine basked in this as well:

> The whole redeemed community, that is the congregation and society of saints, is the universal sacrifice offered to God through the great high-priest, Who offered Himself in His passion for us, so that we might be the body of so great a Head ... When then the Apostle exhorteth us to present our bodies as a living victim ... this is the sacrifice of Christians: we who are many are one body in Christ. The Church celebrates it in the sacrament of the altar which is so familiar to the faithful, in which is shown that in what she offers she herself is offered.[5]

That is the priesthood of all believers and it is the priesthood of men and women. If anything, this sacrificial act, the offering of our bodies with vigor before the Lord, is allegorically feminine since it is the song of Mary resung and echoes the song of all creation to the beauty of the Creator.

But Christ has not commanded us just to face God with our offering; He has commanded certain men to do special things in His name, to represent Him before the people, to face the people with His offering to them. The specially ordained priest, presiding at the Eucharist, is not Fr. Smith or Fr. Jones; he is a man, alter-Christus, in the divine economy in which the Christus was a man.

> ... it is an old saying in the army that you salute the uniform not the wearer. Only one wearing the masculine uniform can (provisionally, and till the Parousia) represent the Lord to the Church: for we are all, corporately and individually, feminine to Him. We men may often make very bad priests. That is because we are insufficiently masculine. It is no cure to call in those who are not masculine at all.[6]

Were the priestly office solely a teaching or administrative office, it would fully be the proper work of women as well as men. It is not definitively such a pastoral office, however. A priest is not only elder or "presbyter," with responsibilities of leadership and direction, he is also *sacerdos,* offeror of God's gift to the people as well as of the people's gift to God. That divine license is the setting apart of certain men to represent, through the consecration of the people's offering of bread and wine, Christ's offering of His Body and Blood. That special office originally was the commission of Christ to His apostles. The fact that its duties, in the sense of sacerdos, are clearly outlined no earlier than the writings of Hippolytus around the early third century probably indicates two things.

First, the priesthood of Christ as mediator between God and man is Christ's alone and any talk of priests in the plural has the danger of detracting from this fundamental point. Second, Christ has delegated His priesthood to earthly representatives but it is indeed only a vicarious office commissioned to the small group of apostles and their successors.

While the institution of the vicarious priesthood of the apostles is historic, its significance was only slowly comprehended. The clear statement that the priest is both presbyter and sacerdos, mediator and offeror of sacrifices, is historically evident but is fundamentally a theological statement. Regardless of what churches may have done with the priesthood its meaning is inviolable.

The common appreciation of the elder as a priest was finally accomplished after the middle of the fourth century. First recognition was still given to the bishops who were directly styled, through their apostolic commission, as sacerdos or *archhiereus.* The local priests or elders had their commission from these bishops or "high-priests," so they were each called *hiereus* or *sacerdos secundi ordinis,*[7] which is quite like saying vice-priest in the sense of vicar. What the bishop is in relation to Christ, so is the priest in relation to his bishop. Each is a representative of the delegating authority. Certain liturgical customs, preserved through the eclecticism of church customary have long symbolized this. Take for example the old practice of the priest's crossed stole alongside the Bishop's uncrossed, or the Bishop's Host called the *fermentum* carried by a deacon, originally in fact and later symbolically, to each priest's mass.

The office of the ordained priest is then demonstrably a representation of Christ before the people by way of apostolic commission through the bishop. The graph of this is the Eucharistic ceremonial becoming common in the Western church. The priest sits in the attitude of the people for the first part of the rite called the *synaxis,* or teaching part. Here he is elder and teacher, and this is the field of the general priesthood of men and women presenting souls and bodies to their Lord Creator. There is nothing in this ante-communion, unless one includes absolution of sins, for which an ordained priest is required. Commencing with the actual Eucharistic celebration, however, the ordained priest assumes a position behind the altar facing the people, no longer one of the people offering their gifts, but Christ facing them and offering Himself through his hands. This is a *particular* priesthood through which Christ is vicariously presented them in the particular forms of bread and wine. The manhood of the priest, and not just his humanity, is as symbolic as the bread and wine, and the Messianic selection of this manly form on the side of a lake or under a fig tree was historically as specific as the choice of bread and wine from the foods on the table in the Upper Room. The priest's sex is as much a symbol of his priesthood as is his stole. In the language of purpose, to change the symbol is aesthetically and theologically illegitimate.

* * *

Symbolism in the above sense is not a subjective matter in any superficial sense. It is a deeper thing than that. Symbols to us are valid only if they do convey an objective meaning; reality is definitively the meaning of a thing. William Temple, in an attempt to satisfy this kind of conscience, suggested what he called "transvaluation" as an alternative to the established way of explaining the real presence of Christ in the Eucharist in the Thomistic terms of transubstantiation. In transvaluation, reality is the inherent meaning of a thing in terms of value. That is a moral category. The value of the Sacrament is that the bread and wine are made the effective presence of Christ among us. Today we have found a new and equally important word: transignification. Reality is the meaning of thing not in terms of its value but of its purpose. Even value is contingent upon what a thing is simply meant to be. It is true that this can lead to the most boringly subjective pre-occupation with what we call "meaningfulness." We have heard that song pattered much in recent years. However, if we understand this "transignification" as divinely and not humanly purposed, if we are ready to yield to what God intends something to mean then we are in the presence of profound reality, pragmatism measured not by efficiency but by truth.

Dr. Quick deals with essentially this same thing using different terms in his book *The Christian Sacraments*.[8] Writing before the construction of Temple's "transvaluation" theory, and of course before "transignification," he speaks of "instrumentality and significance." Instrumentality is concerned with what is done with objects, significance with what is known by them. If our reference is to be that of "transvaluation," we shall tend to think of sacramental objects as "instruments" while under "transfiguration" they more likely called symbols. Both are valid expressions of a common reality.

In speaking of the priesthood, its maleness is understood both in terms of instrumentality, or value, and of significance. Quite simply for the moment, the priest is an instrument of God when he consecrates, or creates; the significance of his maleness in this instrumentality is that it is a symbol of the seminal initiative of God. The instrument and the symbol become one: the priest consecrates at the head of the people because God has singled out him in his maleness to be Christ for the people, the summation of the naked man before his mother on Golgotha and the whitely robed man before the harlot in the Garden. Sex and Eucharist are together; the priest with an "identity crisis" will most usually be the priest who does not understand that his central job is to be a man at the altar.

* * *

The historic evidence is that God is much concerned with making the meaning of things clear to us. That is why we have the sacramental symbols. If we are perceptive, we can appreciate God's conveyance of meaning in many more symbols than those traditionally assigned to the seven sacramental categories officially defined in the twelfth century. A hundred years before that Peter Damian was seeing symbols everywhere. In a powerful sense, for example, an engagement ring in the local jeweller's window and St. Edward's Crown in the Tower of London are sacramental symbols. The Eastern mind is far more sensitive to these things than we. In the Orthodox tradition a world of crafted objects, and most specifically icons, are symbols of divine realities. More importantly, through "transignification" they convey to us the reality of what they symbolize. An engagement ring worn on a finger is the betrothal itself; a crown on an anointed head is the monarchy itself; and an icon of Our Lady of the Sign, painted with prayer and set apart with incense and blessing, is the actual reality of the Incarnation promised by Isaiah in his vision of Theotokos, the Holy Mother. So, the image of Christ's face which on Veronica's veil in Western tradition serves for our edification and curiosity as to what Jesus looked like, becomes in Eastern wisdom the icon of God the Father, God "in the face of Christ," because that is really what Christ means: the visible presence of God who always was and who climbed the heavens ever before He climbed the hills of Galilee.

The priest is the icon of Christ. Just as Christ's meaning is Emmanuel, God with Us, so is the priest Christ with Us. A word of caution is needed: the danger of likening Christ to an icon is that we might conclude he is the reality of God only because he was set apart to be this thing; that error is adoptionism, the belief that Christ originally was nothing but human and then God entered Him at a certain moment in His life. Quite otherwise, Christ existed before all worlds and was divine as a baby as he was in the Easter garden. Thus we must speak cautiously of the icon Christ and so with the icon priest. The priest is not made a priest by his ordination. That is his birthgift in baptism. What ordination does is set apart certain of the priestly race to represent in the color and line of their person, or what we call their sex, the form and reality of Christus Pantocrator, creator of all things, who was also Deus Incarnatus; in priestly iconography the male sex is as vital as every rule about line and composition in formal iconography. The priest is in an awful way, through the breath of God and the Amen of the people, a way so awful that for any man with a mind it must cause embarrassment, the reality of the Incarnation confronting us at the altar. It has nothing to do with the worthiness of the priest as the Donatist heretics in fourth century Africa tried to assert. Some of the world's most venerated icons are pretty maudlin works of art; so are priests often not gainly proofs of manhood. Nor does it in anyway suggest the superiority of male over female in the order of creation. We have gone all over that. The priestly act is verified by the Amen of all Christian people, male and female. It is an Amen to an act powered by God and charged to certain persons who, because of the fact of sex, have a particular responsibility in creation.

We have spoken of all Christians as priests. As Father Huntington, founder of the Order of the Holy Cross, was dying in a New York hospital with all the city driving on outside, he took a friend's hand and said, "Tell them I love them and I shall always love them; tell them I am praying for them and I shall always pray for them." Then, with both hands free, he raised them as did Aaron in the desert and Jesus on the cross and said,

"I am lifting up hands of intercession for them; I shall always intercede for them."[9] This is the priesthood of all believers; it is the priestly chant of all those women and men from the street-women and thieves to the Mother of God, on earth and in heaven, who have been called to stand before the Lord.

The great Dr. Liddon said in one of his University Sermons:

> Certainly if Christian laymen would only believe with all their hearts that they are really priests, we should very soon escape from some of the difficulties which vex the Church of Christ. For it would then be seen that in the Christian Church the difference between clergy and laity is only a difference of the degree in which certain spiritual powers are conferred; that it is not a difference of kind. Spiritual endowments are given to the laymen with one purpose, to the Christian minister with another: the object of the first is personal, that of the second is corporate . . . [10]

The only qualification here is one which R. C. Moberly makes: namely, that the absence of "difference in kind" does not mean that there is no difference in function.[11] The ordained priest sums up in his action the priestly authority of all believers. His particular priestly authority comes not from what he can do in and of himself from what he knows, but from the acknowledgement of the people that Christ has willed him to be in his person in their midst what the people are collectively: the body of Christ. This is why the priest is ordained and set apart. He is not made different in kind from the people; to make him different in kind would be to deny his priesthood since the people are priests, just as we deny the divine relation of Christ and the father when we say they are not of the same substance. The relation between the particular priest and all believers is like that between the Son and the father: their substance is the same so that we may say the ordination of a priest is not a creation but a begetting. The reason the priest is set apart is that his function is different; his function is to represent *to the people* the Christ who is in each of them by creating, or consecrating, with the consent of the people and the power of

Creation. Its edge has such wonder that it is the breath of God upon His Beloved, courted through all the desert walks, married on the cross. Only Narcissus, the superstitious empiricist, could look at this water and see nothing but himself.

God calls Himself a man because He has taken a bride and so He has chosen men to be His hands at the head of the table. This will dismay many because most of us are not pagan enough to be good Christians. We prefer the common rooms "reeking with logic," the eminent sensibleness of a God we elect to protect our rights, who strides but does not dance, who likes but does not love. Then let us build altars to a Supreme Being and sing the neutral song of the Celebration of Life. That will not, of course, solve things. Someone will manage to catch a spark from Easter and see a Gardener, a Rabbi, a Man staring at His Creation. And in this world all who stand near will see fully high and fully wide the way of a Man with a Maiden.

NOTES

CHAPTER I

1. "The Daily" (Newspaper of the General Convention of the Episcopal Church), October 13, 1970.
2. Samuel Butler: "Hudibras," 11.1277ff.
3. Kathleen Bliss: *The Service and Status of Women in the Churches* (London: SCM Press, 1952) p. 133.
4. cf. Rom. XVI:1; 1 Tim. iii.8ff.
5. cf. Gerald Vann: *Morals and Man,* p. 172. New York: Sheed and Ward, 1960.
6. Thomas Merton: *Theoria to Theory,* Vol. 2. 1st quarter. October, 1967.
7. William Law: *A Serious Call to a Devout and Holy Life,* p. 94. Philadelphia: Westminster Press 1965.
8. C. S. Lewis: *God in the Dock,* p. 234; originally in *Time and Tide,* vol. XXIX (August 14, 1948) ed. Walter Hooper, Grand Rapids: William B. Eerdmans, 1970.
9. *Ibid.*
10. D. H. Lawrence, *Apropos,* p. 65., cf. Vann. pp. 174-5.
11. Col. 2:8.

CHAPTER II

1. "The Daily" cit.
2. Five Books in Reply to Marcion, ii.258-99.
3. Alden D. Kelley: *The People of God*, Greenwich: Seabury Press, 1962, p. 107.
4. Simon de Beauvoir, in "The New York Times Magazine," July 11, 1971, p. 38.
5. Matthew Arnold, "The New Sirens" (in R. V. Johnson: *Aestheticism*, p. 40).
6. H. F. Rall in Kepler: *Contemporary Thinking about Paul,* p. 280.
7. 1 Cor. 11:3.
8. Karl Rahner: "The Month," May 1971, Vol. ccxxxi, No. 1245, p. 137.

9. Gal. 3:28.
10. John 17:21.

CHAPTER III

1. W. H. Auden: "The Meditation of Simeon", London: Faber & Faber, Ltd., 1944.
2. cf. Immanuel Kant: *Critique of Judgement* (New York: Habner: 1966).
3. Xenophon, *Memorabilia,* III viii:4-7 (quoted) in Edmund Burke: *A Philosophical Enquiry into the Origin of Our Ideas,* ed. J. I. Boulton, London: 1958.
4. St. Augustine: *De Doctr, Christ.,* I. IV:24-26
5. Col. 2:15.
6. In speaking of the "discriminatory" factor in Christ's commissioning of the apostles, it must be pointed out that their exclusive maleness is a matter different from their exclusive Jewishness; Christ did choose twelve Jewish men but the argument that the opening of the priesthood to non-Jews justifies the opening of it to women as well cannot be maintained. Inasmuch as Christ meant all baptised persons to be New Israelites, baptism confers authentic covenant Jewishness upon all persons, thus actually fulfilling the symbolic religious requirements. This alteration of the definition of what constitutes children of the Covenant is permitted by specific Scriptural authority through the Council of Jerusalem, Peter's baptism of Cornelius, the testimony of Paul, etc. The exemption of Christians from specific Levitical obedience and indeed from all religious and racial qualifications has no parallel in any Scriptural exemptions from maleness and femaleness which, if anything, are reaffirmed as realities divinely intended and blessed. To suggest that sex plays no greater role than religion or race in personal formation is contrary to psychological reality. A post-Freudian world recognizes that religious and racial factors mold the individual *per accidens* while sex is part of the very *esse* of a human. Race and religion are normal, evolutionary phenomena but sexuality is a constant, always divided by two and always real despite the vicissitudes of religion and race.
7. Moberly: *The Minsterial Priesthood,* p. 61, New York: Longmans, Green & Co. 1910.

CHAPTER IV

1. Walter Pater: *The Renaissance,* New York: The New American Library, 1949, p. 149.
2. Hosea 11.
3. John 2:4; John 19:26.
4. Eric L. Mascall: "The Ministry of Women," a letter in *Theology,* Vol. LVII, No. 413 (November 1954), p. 428.
5. E. O. James in *The American Church News,* Summer, 1971, pp. 3ff.

CHAPTER V

1. cf. John Jay Hughes: *Absolutely Null and Utterly Void,* Washington Corpus Books, 1968.
2. J. N. D. Kelly: *Early Christian Doctrine,* New York: Harper and Row, 1958, p. 51.
3. John Macquarrie: *Principles of Christian Theology*, New York: Charles Scribner's Sons, 1966, p. 386.
4. Lewis: *God in the Dock, op. cit.,* p. 336.
5. J. H. Newman: *Apoligia pro Vita Sua,* New York: Longman, Green & Co., 1947, p. 94.

CHAPTER VI

1. In Henru de Lubac, *The Splendour of the Church,* p. 30, Glen Rock: Deus Press 1956.
2. James B. Simpson and Edward M. Story: *The Long Shadows of Lambeth X*, New York: McGraw Hill, 1969, pp. 189-90.
3. *Church Times,* London: June 27, 1971.

CHAPTER VII

1. Article XX, Articles of Religion; *The Book of Common Prayer*
2. *Commonweal,* Vol. XCIV No. 14, June 25, 1971.
3. cf. Dr. E. O. James, *op. cit.*
4. David Jenkins: *The Glory of Man* (Bampton Lectures for 1966) London: 1967, p. 45.

5. Moberly, *op. cit.*, p. 144.
6. *Dutch Cathechism*, p. 363. New York: Herder & Herder, 1967.
7. Macquarrie, *op. cit.*, pp. 386-7.
8. J. B. Higgins: "1 Timothy," ed. T. W. Manson: "Romans" in *Peake's Commentary on the Bible*, ed. Matthew Black, London: Thomas Nelson, 1962.
9. Moberly, *op. cit.*, p. 140.
10. *Constitutions of the Holy Apostles in the Ante-Nicene Fathers*, Vol. VII, Book iii, Sec. vi, p. 427.
11. cf. Dorothy Musgrave Arnold: *Dorothy Kerin*, London: Hodder & Stoughton, 1965.

CHAPTER VIII

1. cf. Donald Baillie, *God was in Christ*, New York: Charles Scribner's Sons, 1948, p. 71. note.
2. *Ibid.*
3. C. S. Phillips: *The Church in France 1789-1848*, London: A. R. Mowbray and Co., Ltd., p. 33.
4. 2 Samuel 6:21.
5. David McClelland, in *The Ministry and Mental Health*, New York: Association Press, 1960, p. 55.
6. Baillie, *op. cit.*, p. 132.
7. Matthew 28:13.
8. Eph. 5:32.
9. cf. Hughell Fosbroke: *God in the Heart of Things*, Greenwich: Seabury Press 1962, p. 108.
10. *Paradise Lost*, L. 423.
11. 1 Cor. 13:12.
12. cf. Charles Williams: *The Figure of Beatrice*, London: Faber & Faber, 1943, p. 212.
13. F. R. Barry: *Secular and Supernatural*, London: SCM Press, pp. 148-149.

14. C. H. Dodd: *The Authority of the Bible*, London: Fontana Books, 1960, p. 255.
15. Gerardus van der Leeuw: *Sacred and Profane Beauty: the Holy in Art*, New York: Abingdon Press, 1963, p. 310.

CHAPTER IX

1. Louis Bouyer: *Dieu Vivant*, p. 140 (cf., de Lubac, *op. cit.*, p. 53).
2. Yves Congar: *Lay People in the Church*, tr. Donald Attwater, London: Bloomsbury Publishing Company, 1957.
3. Robert Browning: "The Ring and the Book," L. 1056.
4. "The Holy Communion," *Book of Common Prayer*.
5. St. Augustine: *De civitate dei*, 10, 6.
6. C. S. Lewis, *op. cit.*, p. 461.
7. Gregory Dix: *The Shape of the Liturgy*, London: Dacre Press, 1970, p. 34.
8. Oliver Chase Quick: *The Christian Sacraments*, London: Nisbet and Company, 1927, ch. 1.
9. V. Scudder: *Father Huntington*, New York: Dutton & Company, 1940, pp. 366-367.
10. cf. Moberly, *op. cit.*, p. 96.
11. *Ibid.*
12. Evelyn Underhill: *The Mystery of Sacrifice*, London: Longmans, Green & Company, 1948, pp. 43-44.
13. Nicholas Berdyaev: *The Destiny of Man*, London: G. Bles, The Century Press, 1937, p. 166.
14. *Summa Theologica* III, q. 80 a.12, ad.3.

DATE DUE

JUN 2 '78			
JUL 1 0 '89			
GAYLORD			PRINTED IN U.S.A.